MARVEL EDUCATION

A CLASSROOM MANAGEMENT GUIDE FOR NEW EDUCATORS AND ANYONE SERIOUS ABOUT TEACHING IN URBAN HIGH SCHOOLS

EMIR CRUZ FERNÁNDEZ

© **Copyright 2023 - All rights reserved.**

The content within this book may not be reproduced, duplicated or transmitted without direct written permission from the author or the publisher.

Under no circumstances will any blame or legal responsibility be held against the publisher or author for any damages, reparation, or monetary loss due to the information contained within this book, either directly or indirectly.

Legal Notice:

This book is copyright protected. It is only for personal use. You cannot amend, distribute, sell, use, quote or paraphrase any part of the content within this book, without the consent of the author or publisher.

Disclaimer Notice:

Please note the information contained within this document is for educational and entertainment purposes only. All effort has been executed to present accurate, up to date, reliable, complete information. No warranties of any kind are declared or implied. Readers acknowledge that the author is not engaged in the rendering of legal, financial, medical or professional advice. The content within this book has been derived from various sources. Please consult a licensed professional before attempting any techniques outlined in this book.

By reading this document, the reader agrees that under no circumstances is the author responsible for any losses, direct or indirect, that are incurred as a result of the use of the information contained within this document, including, but not limited to, errors, omissions, or inaccuracies.

❦ Created with Vellum

CONTENTS

Introduction   5

1. THE POWER OF PRESENCE: INSPIRING STUDENTS TO LISTEN AND ENGAGE   13
   Why Students Don't Listen   14
   Awakening Limitless Horizons   16
   Disruptive Behavior in Schools   21
   Your Role as a Teacher   24
   Cracking the Code of Student Disruption: A Powerful Insight   27

2. IGNITING THE SPARK OF MOTIVATION   31
   The Lack of Motivation in Students   33
   Ready to Elevate Your Classroom? Unleash the Power of Motivation!   39
   When Motivation Is Not Enough   41
   Unleashing Student Motivation for Marvelous Learning   44
   Awakening Your Teacher Genius: The Marvelous Act of Self-Motivation   45

3. FROM PURPOSELESSNESS TO PURPOSEFULNESS: CULTIVATING MEANING   47
   Empowering Through the Art of Questioning   48
   The Need for Purpose   52
   Authentic Identity   55
   Unleashing the Secrets to Students' Authenticity: The Marvelous Path to Self-Discovery   60

4. THE MYTHIC MARVEL: EMPOWERING EDUCATION THROUGH STORYTELLING   67
   My Understanding of Myths   69
   Four Functions of Myths   71
   Teens Develop Their Identities through Personal Myth   79
   Empowered Education: My Personal Mythic Way   83

5. MARVEL! ... 85
   Awe as a Factor of Well-Being ... 86
   Transcending Limits: The Power of Awe Moments ... 88
   Igniting Wonder: The Power of Awe Moments in the Classroom ... 91
   Awe-Inspired Change ... 95
   Awing Students ... 100

6. SOCRATIC DIALOGUE: UNLEASHING MARVELOUS CLASSROOM CONVERSATIONS ... 105
   Transformative Pedagogy of the Socratic Method ... 109
   Harnessing the Socratic Method for Effective Teaching ... 113
   The Extraordinary Power of Dialogue ... 118

7. THE POWER OF LOVE IN THE CLASSROOM: EMPOWERING STUDENT VOICE AND IDENTITY ... 121
   School as a Venue of Love ... 123
   The Self as a Hero ... 125
   Building Bridges to Success: The Marvel Education Approach ... 129
   Marvelous Love ... 131

   Stepping into Your Marvelous Future ... 135
   References ... 139

INTRODUCTION

> *"Teaching is more than imparting knowledge; it is inspiring change. Learning is more than absorbing facts; it is acquiring understanding."*
>
> — WILLIAM ARTHUR WARD

Data from the National Education Association reveals alarming trends in the American educational system (Walker, 2022). For example, 55 percent of currently employed educators have considered leaving the profession—and this is true of teachers across various age groups, locations, and lengths of time in the field. One of the main reasons for this is that the United States is facing a shortage of teachers in our schools. That shortage is growing worse every year. The overall number of teachers in public schools has decreased by 600,000 from 2020 to 2022, and is expected to decrease even more in 2023.

This teacher shortage causes a ripple effect throughout the entire school system. Some teachers report that they are overworked. Others say that the number of students they are assigned per class has increased without consideration of the time and effort needed to manage a classroom. In addition, "safety concerns, low salaries, funding deficits, and declining mental health, are not new issues—but the ongoing Covid-19 pandemic has intensified existing problems within the profession" (Smith, 2022).

Even with federal and state governments writing bills, granting funding for programs, and other private and public initiatives, it is safe to say that the educational system is going through a crisis—a crisis on a scale we've never seen before. This situation has led to educators having some of the highest burnout rates among professionals. There simply is not enough being done to address these problems. If you think the numbers are not as significant as they seem, here are a few others to consider, according to Harris (2023):

- 81 percent of teachers interviewed claim their workload has increased, and 55 percent said they would leave the profession because of it.
- 65 percent of teachers claim they have experienced negative physical and mental health repercussions because of excessive workloads.
- 46 percent of teachers work more than fifty hours per week, including the time they are at the education center plus the hours they dedicate to the profession at home.

- When sleep is concerned, 11 percent of the teachers claim to suffer from insomnia and have issues sleeping, while the other 32 percent say that they sleep less than six hours every night.
- 57 percent of these professionals say they do not have time for anything else, not even a social life, apart from the activities they do for school.
- Furthermore, 58 percent claim they are always tired, leading to at least 36 percent affirming that they get irritated at home and school most days.

Once you consider these statistics, it becomes easy to understand why the educational system as we know it is suffering. These circumstances lead teachers to take more days off, which leaves students without the sense of security and continuity they need for a successful school year. Furthermore, the high burdens placed on teachers make it nearly impossible for them to achieve a healthy work-life balance. The stress of these challenges makes it more likely for teachers to leave and fewer to join this marvelous profession.

Even aside from school professionals being understaffed and overworked, there are more factors to consider. Too often, we find a lack of structure in schools, and teachers who have received little to no training when they begin working in the classroom. If you've experienced these problems firsthand and feel like you're at the end of your rope, I understand how you're feeling. I have been there, and I can relate to what you're going through. But are we ready to give up on our younger generations because the system does not help us? Are we satisfied with leaving the futures of our children and teenagers in the hands of unprepared professionals? Lastly, are you ready to leave a profession you love and have dedicated your life to?

I hope not. And I hope that this book helps you see that not all is lost. I want to show you that there are solutions to these problems. There are ways to be successful in the classroom despite the challenges you face.

EMPOWERMENT STARTS WITH YOU: UNLOCKING OUR TEACHER BRILLIANCE

As a new teacher in New York City's public schools, I discovered that the reality of teaching was vastly different from what I had learned in college. Almost immediately upon entering the classroom, I sensed that I was unprepared. Without proper guidance or training in classroom management, I felt lost. However, this ignited a sense of purpose in me to uncover the hidden treasures of effective classroom management. Drawing from my firsthand experiences, I will share the secrets that can guide you along an inspired path to create a positive learning environment for your students.

Thrown into the deep end without proper training or guidance, I discovered that experience is the greatest teacher. Through trial and error, I learned to navigate the choppy waters of classroom management. With over two decades of experience, I'm thrilled to now share the tools and strategies that have transformed my classroom into a place of wonder and inspiration. With the right mindset and approach, you can create a learning environment that fosters growth, creativity, and joy for you and your students.

Join me on a transformative journey in *Marvel Education*, where I will equip you with the tools to overcome your classroom management challenges. I will show you how to bring meaning to your lessons using the power of myths. Together, we will explore the root causes of disruptive behavior and create an inspiring learning environment. By embracing the principles outlined in this book, you will unlock your potential as a teacher and empower your students to achieve their greatest potential.

Marvel Education is not just a classroom management guide. It is also a roadmap to reignite your passion for teaching and reclaim your purpose. Let this guide empower you with the tools and inspiration you need to thrive as an educator. Journey through these pages and rediscover the joy of shaping young minds and positively impacting their lives. Let's create a classroom where students can flourish and reach their full potential.

As a teacher in one of the world's largest cities, I've experienced the challenges and hardships that come with working in public schools. However, through my journey, I've learned that change is always possible, and it starts with you. You have the power to transform your classroom into a space of inspiration and positivity, no matter the students' backgrounds or circumstances. By tapping into your inner strength and following the guidance in this book, you can overcome burnout and create a learning environment that fosters growth and success for both you and your students.

Discover the transformational power of *Marvel Education* and unlock the boundless potential you have as an educator. Open your mind to new possibilities and witness the incredible changes that can occur. With this journey, you will gain insights and tools to overcome the most challenging aspects of classroom management and become a beacon of light for your students. Let's create a classroom environment where anything is possible and unlock the power of change together.

Dear fellow educator, let's awaken the hero within and embrace our power to inspire change. You have been called to this noble profession for a reason—to make a positive impact on young minds and transform children's lives. You may face daunting challenges in the classroom, but fear not, for you are not alone. I am here to guide and empower you on your journey toward greatness. Together, let's unlock the secrets to creating a classroom where students thrive and achieve their dreams. Your time has come to shine and make a difference. Let's make it happen!

DISCOVER THE MARVELS OF CLASSROOM MANAGEMENT: WHAT AWAITS YOU IN THIS BOOK

With experience teaching in public high schools, community colleges, and universities, I understand the challenges you face in the classroom. In this book, I'll share personal tips and ideas that have worked for me and encourage you to explore your own creativity and potential. In this book, I will remind you of all the positive things education brings to teachers, to students, and to society as a whole. I will talk about the challenge of motivation, as well as some of our most common problems, and provide solutions that have worked for me and fellow educators. In each example or anecdote used in this book, the names of students have been changed to protect their privacy.

As we embark on this journey together, I ask you to have faith in your own power to create a positive change in your classroom. Let's believe in our ability to transform the chaotic public school systems and inspire the next generation of leaders. By recognizing the unique qualities of each student, we can create a classroom environment where everyone thrives. Never forget that you have the power to make a difference, and together, we can light up the path toward a brighter future.

It is vital to emphasize that the experiences and techniques shared here are not rigid blueprints applicable to all situations. Instead, this book aims to inspire and empower, guiding you toward your own unique path as an educator in urban high schools. The anecdotes, examples, and stories within these pages are drawn from my authentic encounters, but it is essential to acknowledge that each teacher possesses customized approaches. The insights offered here are honed through years of dedicated practice, requiring the cultivation of skills and experiential wisdom the new teacher will undoubtedly acquire or develop. Embrace the openness to expand your repertoire, for it is through this expansive embrace that you will navigate the rich tapestry of urban education's vast ocean.

I urge you to keep your mind open on this journey, and remember what brought you to this profession in the first place. *Marvel Education* invites you to embrace the transformative potential of your students, of your school, and the power that exists in you. As you read this guide, please leave behind any doubts or fears you may have developed during your career. Instead, allow yourself to be inspired by what is possible. Are you ready to join me on this journey?

1

THE POWER OF PRESENCE: INSPIRING STUDENTS TO LISTEN AND ENGAGE

 *"I am not a teacher, but an awakener."*

— ROBERT FROST

Do you ever feel overwhelmed by the challenge of managing your students? You're not alone. But don't give up hope, because you can turn things around and create a thriving classroom environment.

In this chapter, we'll explore the power of presence, which can help you create a learning environment that inspires your students to listen and engage. By mastering the art of presence, you'll learn how to connect with your students on a deeper level and foster a sense of community in your classroom.

As educators, we may sometimes need guidance on how to maintain focus in the classroom, especially when students seem disinterested or unresponsive. But keep pursuing your dream of inspiring your students to become incredible human beings. There are solutions, and I am excited to reveal them to you. Are you ready to unlock your full potential as a teacher and create a classroom that inspires your students to learn and grow? Let's get started!

WHY STUDENTS DON'T LISTEN

To start, you first need to understand **what** is happening and **why** your students aren't listening. Some reasons might be about them, but others may be about you. When was the last time you examined what you are teaching and saw that it was fun and engaging?

Take a moment to reflect: Do you remember what it was like in the classroom when you were in school? You probably had a favorite teacher, and one of the reasons you (and probably other students) liked them so much was their ability to captivate your attention by making the subject they were teaching **interesting**. When this happens, no television show, movie release, music, or anything else will keep them from focusing on your class.

Students—especially those exposed to toxic situations at home, in the streets, and in the educational system—can easily overlook how exciting and life-changing learning in the classroom can be. Although teaching has always been a challenging profession, the challenge for the twenty-first century teacher is enormous. We compete with Netflix, YouTube, video games, Disney Plus, social media, and a host of other unprecedented distractions.

In addition to this, teachers who are overworked, overwhelmed, and overloaded just don't feel motivated anymore. **We** are tired. But so are they. Students see going to school as something they must do, because their caregivers are making them do it. In some cases, they have nowhere else to go. What kind of expectations do you think a child or a teenager will have from school from this point of view?

This brings us to one of the primary reasons students don't listen: lack of motivation. Students do not automatically understand why studying, going to school, and learning are so important. Many of them are struggling at home. Why should they see going to school as something that will change their lives? They have **many** questions, and this feeling of uncertainty about the future. What do you think will be the priority if they worry about caring for a parent or a younger sibling and juggling this with their homework?

If this is the case—that problems outside the school are motivating disruptive behaviors—they may not feel seen if you judge them only based on what you see in the classroom. They feel like they are part of a system that does not acknowledge their existence and that you, their teacher, are just here to tell them a bunch of rules, even though you do not understand why they are so tired and unmotivated. Going to school is often their only opportunity to be themselves and express individuality.

As teachers, we have a powerful impact on our students' lives. Sometimes, that impact can manifest as disruptive behavior, chatter, and disinterest in our lessons. But consider this:

imagine just one student struggling in your classroom. Now, picture ten more, just like them. It's easy to see why chaos can reign. However, you entered this profession as a teacher to make a difference. You can transform these challenging situations and inspire your students to reach their full potential. Let's explore how to do just that and create a positive and productive classroom environment.

To connect with your students, listen to them. What are they trying to communicate? What message are they trying to convey to you? While this level of analysis may not be part of your official job description, it can still lead you to make a difference in their lives. Why did you become a teacher? You have the power to be the change you wish to see. Listen to their message, and you may be surprised at how much easier it becomes to teach them once they feel heard and understood.

AWAKENING LIMITLESS HORIZONS

When you think about **what** you can do to help these students pay attention in class, you must consider that you are fighting an entire system. You are going against difficult administrators, a toxic school environment, parents who sometimes do not care, and numerous other variables that are standing between that student and the quality education they need. It is time to "put your thinking cap on," as I would often say to my students, and start looking for solutions. What can you do to show these students that being in school will benefit them, even if they cannot see it right now?

Here are a few things you can do to help improve communication in the classroom and make your students want to listen to what is being said:

1. Look into yourself

Unlock effective classroom management by reflecting on personal biases, triggers, and other areas where you can improve as a person. Your behavior and mindset can significantly impact your ability to manage the classroom. Conduct anonymous surveys to gather student feedback and observe your teaching. Adjust and try new techniques to create a learning environment that fosters growth. Appreciate students' efforts, listen to their feedback, and show them the possibilities of what they can achieve. Create a positive and successful classroom experience together.

2. Establish a routine

From day one, inform your students of your teaching approach and structure. Set up a solid system that helps them identify what comes next without constant guidance. This creates a stable and predictable learning environment to help your students thrive. As Meredith (2019) suggested, "Set up systems that are so solid they implement themselves." A well-structured classroom routine enables students to seamlessly go from activity to activity.

3. Reinforce expectations

After establishing a routine, communicate your expectations to your students. This agreement involves your commitment to guide and teach them while they agree to listen and be respectful. Share your desired behavior, engagement, and listening, and how they should carry out assigned tasks (Mustafa, 2023a). Make it a conversation by asking about their expectations and what they want from the class. Set classroom rules together and remind them when these expectations are not met. Having a mutual understanding creates a positive learning environment for everyone.

4. Control the narrative

As a teacher, your primary focus is on teaching, not just managing behavior. Controlling the narrative is essential to create a positive classroom environment, but not at the expense of your student's participation. When you set the tone for how the class should run and actively listen to students' feedback, you can create a more collaborative and empowering learning environment. This will help your students feel valued, which, in turn, will increase their motivation and willingness to cooperate.

5. Build connections

A teacher who fails to connect with their students has little chance of success. You can foster relationships in various ways, such as sharing relatable stories or using engaging teaching techniques. By understanding the needs and demands of your classroom, you can adjust your teaching style to connect with your students. Consider what made you listen to your teachers and what inspired you, then use those elements in your teaching. Building connections with your students can increase their motivation and help them learn more effectively.

6. Listen

No one likes to be ignored. Students may come from an environment where their needs are unmet. In those cases, their need to be heard isn't just a classroom management issue, but also a deeply personal one. You can make a big difference in their lives by actively listening to them without judgment, and showing comprehension of their troubles. This can help establish common ground and a closer relationship over time. Be bold, ask questions, and speak to them privately in the classroom if needed. Listening to students can be a powerful way to support and empower them.

7. Keep your promises

Some students may feel unmotivated if teachers consistently make promises they don't keep. Others may not listen if they don't see any consequences for their actions. It's crucial to keep your promises, whether they are allowing group activities or offering homework incentives. Establishing boundaries and being consistent with your words will earn their respect and show them that you mean what you say. Honoring your commitments will create a positive learning environment where students feel valued and motivated to learn.

8. Appreciate their efforts

People tend not to listen to those who do not appreciate them. They become defensive, dismissive, and indifferent to what you have to say. Do not hold out on praise where it is due. Show your students that they are doing a good job and that, independent of what others may think, they can do a good job and feel appreciated. This will motivate them to complete the assignments, participate, and listen to your lesson.

9. Illuminate possibilities

Some students may struggle to see the opportunities that education can offer, leading them to disengage. As their teacher, it's your role to shine a light on those possibilities and help them navigate their educational path. Education has the power to open doors to opportunities that were previously out of reach. When you show someone a path to success that they couldn't see before, you are offering them a powerful gift.

10. Break the habit

While sometimes the problem may be with us, in other cases, the issue might be that the students were never taught how to behave in a classroom. By actively teaching students to listen and pay attention, you will be breaking habits that would otherwise affect their ability to learn for years to come. Of course, you can expect pushback in these situations. However, it is up to you to reinforce the rules and standards of conduct you set in your classroom.

Several techniques can help students listen to you in creating a harmonious classroom environment. However, it's important to remember that there is no one-size-fits-all solution. To help your students listen to you, it's essential to understand their issues and any external factors affecting them. As Holiday (2018) aptly states, discovering the "why" is key to finding practical solutions. Finding the "why" behind their behavior will make matching the "right" solution easier. Additionally, showing them the importance of school can motivate them to participate and engage in class.

DISRUPTIVE BEHAVIOR IN SCHOOLS

A disruptive behavior in the classroom consists of those that "impede learning and teaching and have the potential to escalate or spread if left unchecked." (Tarr, 2006). Psychologists have been studying classroom behavior for a long time, and there are several theories and studies to help teachers better manage a classroom. Let me be the first to admit that some of them will work and others won't—this will depend on your approach, the students, the context, and several other factors that can impact classroom behavior. However, I want to share something that Youki Terada (2019) presented, discussing the impact of discipline in the classroom.

In the 1950s, psychologists Jacob Kounin and Paul Gump discovered a curious side effect of discipline: If a student was being disruptive and the teacher responded with strict disciplinary measures, the student might stop—but other students would start exhibiting the same misbehavior. Kounin and Gump called this the "ripple effect," and it demonstrated that efforts to control a classroom can backfire (para. 1).

Have you ever experienced this ripple effect in your classroom when trying to control the group after disciplinary measures? If you have, then you know what I mean. This behavior is especially characteristic of teenagers who want to test the limits and see if you will impose the same consequences on them. When this happens, you need to establish control of the classroom by restating the rules and expectations you agreed to at the beginning of the year. Reminding them of these is always a good alternative, but it is only a palliative measure. You will need to identify **why** these disruptive behaviors are happening and the underlying cause for them.

If I were to tell you reasons why students become disruptive, the list would be very long. As a teacher, you have probably seen the most varied motives for this to happen. From a single insect seen in the classroom to a person passing by the door, even the smallest things can break students' concentration. However, a few things can be done to ensure that the disruptions remain as infrequent and insignificant as possible.

The first thing I would say is that you should get to know your students. Sometimes, distraction stems from a student having issues with the content you are presenting to them. The subject may be too hard for them; they may not understand a particular word or concept, or alternatively, a student may get bored if the material seems redundant or too easy. These are very common issues in the classroom, especially when dealing with students from different backgrounds and different levels of commitment to their studies. You must always keep in mind that each student may have received a different level of education, and some might not even understand the language you are speaking. These differences may be especially apparent if you are teaching in a large urban area.

In light of these differences, learning **why** a student may be talking, moving about, or distracting a friend becomes especially important. The first step is to observe before you rush to judgment or discipline. If you still cannot find the cause, it might be worth a try to speak to the student privately. Ask them what you can do to improve his or her learning experience. They might open up to you if you have worked on establishing a relationship with them. On the other hand, I do not recommend calling them out in public and in front of their classmates. Not only will this embarrass them, it can also make them confrontational, bringing even more disruption to the classroom.

Once you can pinpoint the problem, it will be time to establish the strategy you will apply to the classroom. "Strategies for establishing, maintaining, and restoring relationships—such as regular check-ins and focusing on solutions instead of problems—can reduce disruptions by up to 75 percent." (Terada, 2019). Since it is in your best interests to keep the class under control, I suggest you **take it upon yourself** to make the changes and adapt to what the class needs.

This might include adopting a more flexible style, adapting the language and the material to reach students of all levels, and changing the seating arrangement of the class. You should also keep in mind that reinforcing positive behaviors in students is often far more effective than criticizing misbehavior. And look: Don't play favorites. When giving praise and reprimands alike, treat everyone as if they are equal. You should set a bar of what is acceptable and what is not. Punishing one student for something they have done without doing the same for others may make you lose credibility with the class.

If you ever feel like you are about to lose control, think about why you became a teacher in the first place—the wonders of preparing human beings for their future and what they can do. Try not to yell or lose control; excuse yourself for a moment if you have to. Students who can perceive that their teachers are losing control of the class and their feelings tend to escalate the situation. It will be important to ask yourself: What is my role here as their teacher? What can I add to their lives? How can I make this experience noteworthy and positive for them?

YOUR ROLE AS A TEACHER

When trying to figure out a student and the source of what they've learned so far, their parents or caretakers are a logical place to look. These individuals are most likely to be your students' role models. With that said, the amazing thing about being their teacher is that you are probably very high up on their list of influences. Oftentimes, you are second or third after a student's primary caretakers. Schoolteachers play a profound role in shaping a young person's knowledge of the world, in helping them to identify their own capabilities, and in guiding them as they learn to establish their earliest relationships. Can you see how important your job is? You are a role model and often an inspiration to students.

It has been a long time since an educator's only job was to introduce content to students in the classroom. Before, students were seen as passive consumers of information. What they learned should be absorbed without question, and the teacher was seen as a high and unerring authority. Teachers could not deviate from the lessons and methods established by the schools and had to adhere to strict regulations and policies established by the schools they worked in. Children weren't seen as unique individuals. Instead, they were a mass of empty vessels into which content should be deposited as efficiently as possible.

However, information evolved, and things changed. In came the Internet, and information was suddenly available everywhere. Learning was everywhere! According to *The 7 Roles of a Teacher* (n.d.), "Learning is no longer confined to the classroom setting. It occurs at home, in the community, and in the digital and physical world." Classrooms became more open to questions and adopted different teaching methodologies, allowing teachers and students to learn differently.

Today, due to technological and structural changes in our society, finding content is easier than it has ever been. Students no longer need to "cram" in the library or depend on a teacher to learn things. This has led to a significant change in the educator's role in the lives of those who attend their classroom.

Teachers have increased importance in the lives of these youngsters and in determining the adults they will become. Teachers are able to validate or verify information that students may find on the Internet by using their acquired knowledge. Think, for example, about how science teachers can make the connection between what the students see in the classroom and how this can apply to their daily lives. Think about how giving practical examples can help students develop different perspectives on various subjects, such as math. As we will see in Chapter 4, there is a whole "myth" about what teachers do and the model they become to their students.

Consider the role that teachers are adopting outside the classroom. According to Taack Lanier (1997):

> They are working with colleagues, family members, politicians, academics, community members, employers, and others to set clear and obtainable standards for the knowledge, skills, and values we should expect America's children to acquire. They are participating in day-to-day decision making in schools, working side-by-side to set priorities, and dealing with organizational problems that affect their students' learning (para. 25).

Furthermore, when you are a teacher, you can also be a confidant with whom students share details about the personal problems they face at home. You can be a guide that will help the student determine their next steps in life. You need to know that you are changing their lives for the better. You will be even more than a guide and a role model in life; you will show them how to harness knowledge and use it to shape their destiny. And isn't this what it is all about? Revealing, making, and embodying change in this exceptional profession—that's what it means to be an educator.

CRACKING THE CODE OF STUDENT DISRUPTION: A POWERFUL INSIGHT

There was a student I will call Jonas. Jonas was usually violent and foul-mouthed in class. He would refuse to work in class or to submit homework. He would bully other students in the school. I tried different ways to engage him in my lessons, but nothing worked. One day, while riding a train from Manhattan to the Bronx, some guys got on the train car I was in and started dancing wonderfully. Among those dancers, I saw Jonas.

After the performance, the adolescents went around with a hat to collect tips from the passengers. When Jonas saw me among the people, he approached me with a smile and shook my hand. I gave him a small tip, and he said to everyone on the train, "This gentleman you see here is one of the best teachers I ever had. I know I give him a hard time in class, but you should all know I appreciate what he does for me daily." At the moment, I didn't know how to react or what to say. I was a little embarrassed and was not thinking clearly since that public comment was totally unexpected. That day, however, I discovered that Jonas's passion was dancing.

Now that I knew this about Jonas, I had a way to connect with him organically. Since I was an actor, I realized we had a shared love for the performing arts. After that encounter outside the classroom, I would invite him to come to my tutoring period so he could catch up with the material. Jonas started coming to see me for Spanish tutoring. In the process, I discovered that he was homeless. His mother—the only person he felt cared about him—had passed away the previous year. Jonas moved to his father's house to live with his half-siblings and stepmother when his mother passed away. His biological father and stepmother did not care for him.

He did not get along with his siblings, and living with the stepmother was also unbearable, so Jonas gradually moved out of his father's house to live with his hippie friends on the streets of New York City. Many of those friends, like Jonas himself, aspired to be professional dancers one day.

I realized that Jonas's negative attitude toward the class was not personal; he was an adolescent going through a lot. It is essential to highlight that he did not become the most outstanding student in our Spanish course, but he did better in class, and our interaction improved dramatically. It was incredible how his eyes and face shone when he spoke about his greatest passion, dancing.

Knowing that he loved dancing, I often brought up the topic and encouraged him to search for auditions online and professional opportunities as a dancer. At the end of that school year, I accepted a position at a different school. Jonas, a junior when I taught at his school, was supposed to graduate the year I moved. I never saw him again. To this day, I find myself wondering what happened to him and his dream of becoming a dancer.

To finish, I want you to take a moment and think about what you have been doing to change. Have you been going to work to be a role model or a mere transmitter of information? Have you been looking at your students and identifying the real problem? Did you make any attempts to establish or improve communication? I understand that making these demands of yourself can feel like a high, even unreachable, standard—especially if we are new to the field and have just been thrown into the proverbial lion's den. But consider this: If the change does not come from you, where will it come from? What will become of our youth?

2

IGNITING THE SPARK OF MOTIVATION

 "Motivation is the art of getting people to do what you want them to do because they want to do it."

— DWIGHT EISENHOWER

What motivates you daily? Can you remember what motivated you to enter the extraordinary world of education? What keeps you going when it seems that all is lost? **Why** do you keep doing what you are doing?

Motivation is an unstoppable force that drives us toward our dreams and goals. It makes us jump out of bed in the morning with a smile and an eagerness to tackle the day ahead. Without motivation, our lives become dull and uninspiring, and we struggle to progress toward our aspirations. In fact, a lack of motivation can be downright harmful, leading to feelings of despair and hopelessness.

Motivation is essential for teachers' success. Success lies not only in teachers' motivation but also in their ability to motivate students. Motivation ignites passion, leading to engaging lessons and infectious energy. Teachers must encourage students to create a positive learning environment, empowering them to reach their full potential. Teachers and students can create an empowering learning environment together, enabling everyone to learn and grow.

Have you ever noticed that some of your students need the spark of inspiration that drives them to succeed? It's not uncommon for students to feel disconnected from the wonder of education, especially when they are facing challenges at home that can affect their focus. When students lack motivation, it can be like trying to move a mountain with your bare hands—no matter how hard you try, you can't seem to make progress.

But fear not: In this chapter, we will explore the transformative power of motivation and its role in unleashing your students' full potential. Remember when you had a student who didn't want to be there? What did you do? How did you feel? The key to unlocking the potential of these students lies in understanding the root of their lack of motivation and learning how to reignite their inner spark. Through this exploration, we will gain valuable insights into how to inspire even the most unmotivated students to embrace the wonder of education and unlock their full potential.

THE LACK OF MOTIVATION IN STUDENTS

Students who are not motivated do not learn and, therefore, perform poorly in school. Whether this is due to problems within the school (such as bullying or difficulty in understanding the subject) or problems outside the educational environment (such as problems at home), the fact remains that it is hard to be in a classroom with unmotivated students. Even worse, sometimes it seems there is nothing we can do to improve the situation.

Have you ever dealt with a student like this? What did you do? Did you have any success in motivating them? If you did, you likely did the only thing that can help in these situations: Establishing a communication channel and trying to understand why this is happening. Once you do this, the reasons for the lack of motivation appear, and you can act upon it.

However, sometimes communicating with a student is not as easy as it may sound. Students do not always cooperate; for one reason or another, they might be afraid to open up. In that case, it will be essential to observe them and see if there is anything you can learn from their behavior. If you still have doubts, there are some things you can look out for that may help you. Here is a list of some of the most common reasons for lack of motivation in students:

1. Learning disabilities

Sometimes, our students are undiagnosed for cognitive disabilities, intellectual disabilities, or developmental issues. It could be, for example, that the student has ADHD that prevents them from focusing in class and doing their best. When you suspect these cases, you can speak to a professional that can aid you in identifying the optimal approach to help the student and increase their learning abilities (Silva, 2019). This may include adapting the teaching technique and approach for that student with targeted activities. In addition, you must speak with the student's family and the school administration to find the best solutions in these cases.

2. Issues at home

Oftentimes, the problem is not in school or anything related to academics; a student might face problems at home. Some issues, such as parental divorce, family illness, lack of money, and other toxic situations can take away a student's motivation simply because they have other things on their mind. Try thinking about how you would feel under these circumstances. These challenges feel insurmountable to many adults, so imagine how they impact a student who hasn't even left school. These situations increase stress, affecting the child's ability to concentrate in class and stay motivated. In that case, you may notice something wrong if they change their behavior or perform below their normal average. A solution here could be to speak to them and open the communication channel so they feel comfortable confiding in you. The approach does not always need to be direct, however. You can also observe their reactions and discover a solution just by listening.

3. Low academic self-esteem

If you have ever heard a student say, "I don't know, maybe I am just stupid," you may be dealing with low academic self-esteem. In these cases, mostly because of underlying issues, the student might feel that they are not good enough to learn or lack encouragement to continue their journey. Situations like these may require you to offer them tutoring sessions. Use praise to motivate them. Reassure them that they are **not** stupid. Sometimes, low academic self-esteem can be rooted in psychological abuse or neglect outside the classroom. Being generous with praise and ensuring that they feel valued will be essential to motivating them.

4. Lack of role models

If a student comes from a social situation in which there is a lack of role models (or their role models do not value education), this may lead them to be demotivated in the classroom. This is simply because they have no one to look up to when the subject at hand is education. They just can't see the marvel of education and the benefits it will bring, since they have no one to mirror. In this case, you may want to try to identify their interests and show them that they can look up to other people, and that there is no problem with this. Try mentioning some celebrities who have studied and gone to the university despite their "popular" careers. Bring to the classroom other role models they can use as motivation for their future. Also, consider inviting professionals in various fields to your classroom as a way to help students broaden the range of who they view as a role model.

5. Negative teaching environment

The last issue I want to speak about is the fact that some students do not feel that the school is a safe or favorable environment for them. The reasons for this can vary from simple seating chart inadequacy to the ever-worrisome issues with bullying. In these cases, it is essential that you try to identify the source of the problem. Some adjustments may be relatively simple, such as changing the seating organization or being mindful of how you convey the content. Others may be more difficult, such as when you have a student who feels intimidated because they get bullied in the hallway by their peers. In some cases, you may need to make small or subtle adjustments. In the case of bullying, you may need to observe student interactions outside the classroom, since bullies tend to "hide" in front of teachers.

6. Inappropriate teaching method

As we have already seen in the previous chapter, sometimes the problem is with **our approach** to teaching. If we have a class of predominantly active students, one possibility is incorporating more group activities and role-playing with certain subjects. You can also add experiments and other strategies that will give them an alternative to just sitting at their desks and absorbing the content. If this is the case, I suggest you take a poll in the classroom to assess the student's interests, and see what you can do to spike their interest. You don't necessarily need to speak directly about the lesson. You can ask questions about their personalities, interests, and feelings to understand how you can better approach a particular subject and increase classroom motivation.

7. Difficulty understanding the subject

One of the most common reasons why students aren't motivated is the simplest one: They simply don't understand the content you're teaching. In addition to this, they may not see why this content is relevant to their lives. A student like Jonas, for example, might not automatically see how their academics relate to their love of dancing. Showing a dancer how subjects like history or physics apply to dance will help them to be more engaged in the classroom.

8. Low expectations of the future

If you consider the social and economic conditions of some students who attend public schools, you can understand why they expect so little from their future. They may not be motivated because they see no way out of the system and no alternative to improving their lives. This may be even worse if learning is simply not considered essential to success at home. It is here that you, as their teacher, must show them the benefits of learning and how knowledge can change their lives. Motivate them to study. Help them to realize that they can use what they learn to change the future.

9. Too much pressure

Do you remember when you were in school? If you do, you may remember how sometimes there is just too much pressure. We have it from our families, who expect us to perform well. We receive it from our teachers, who want the content to be absorbed. The expectations we set for ourselves can also become burdensome. Think of the overwhelming pressures your students may suffer. In this case, you must try to identify where this pressure is coming from; it might be possible to take action if you determine whether it is coming from you (Are you too demanding in the classroom?) or from the students themselves (Do they put pressure on themselves to excel?). In these cases, you might want to review if you are not being too strict or stern with the class, and find alternatives to help them feel less stressed. Incorporating targeted activities that will help the students feel more at ease or even holding a class outside, for example, can be an alternative to this issue.

As an educator, you may question why motivating students is your responsibility. The answer is simple: It's your obligation to ignite their passion, remind them of **their** potential, and guide **them** to achieve **their** goals. However, what if you're feeling unmotivated yourself? Your **own** inspiration is essential. Recall the passion that drove **you** to teach and the reasons that keep **you** going. Your enthusiasm can spread like wildfire and unlock your students' potential. Let's explore together how motivation matters and how you can catalyze change in your classroom.

READY TO ELEVATE YOUR CLASSROOM? UNLEASH THE POWER OF MOTIVATION!

Motivation is the key to academic success. It's the difference between adequate and inadequate progress, and it starts with belief. Students who believe in themselves show interest in their education and a willingness to learn. Teachers play a vital role in fostering motivation and creating a positive environment. Motivation is a joint effort. We must inspire our students with passion, possibility, and hard work.

When we speak about motivation, we should consider the two types: **intrinsic** and **extrinsic** motivation. The first type involves sources of motivation that begin in the students themselves—their will, their goals, and their determination. This means they are engaged because they are curious, interested, having fun, and have positive feelings toward what is being taught. We see this motivation from students who come from toxic environments and want to change, see the possibility of doing so, and are determined to do so. When this is done, they develop competencies, ask questions in class, plan for the future, and are engaged in what is being done.

On the other hand, extrinsic motivation involves factors outside the student that drive their behaviors. This could include a strong support system at home that encourages a student to continue studying. Another example might be a teacher who presents content in an entertaining and engaging way. Positive or negative reinforcement are two different types of extrinsic motivation. A person can be driven by rewards or praise, or out of a fear of consequences.

External or extrinsic factors may be most evident to you in the school. Intrinsic or internal factors might be most visible in students who exhibit a clear desire to learn, even beyond the in-class instruction. In many cases, it may require more examination on your part to notice all the factors that affect academic performance.

Identifying each student's motivation is not just helpful; it is essential. Or, if they lack it, you can be the motivator by providing extrinsic rewards that will help them see the advantages of being in school. Having a motivated student will benefit everyone. It will increase individual performance, classroom morale, and your own success as a teacher. It is all about what makes them tick.

As educators, we have the power to help students reach their full potential by cultivating a growth mindset. According to Carol Dweck, students with a growth mindset are motivated to see challenges as opportunities for growth. Positive feedback and praise throughout the learning process help keep students engaged and focused on their goals. It's important to remember that every student has the potential for greatness, and it's our responsibility to help them realize it. We can create a nurturing environment that fosters success by embracing a growth mindset and inspiring our students to do the same.

Therefore, I could say that having a motivated student can be essential for your class's success and their learning process. Remember when I mentioned some of the reasons why students do not listen? Well, lack of motivation is one of them, which could potentially lead to disruptive behaviors. On the other hand, a motivated student with a leadership role among their peers will help you have a more pleasant teaching experience with the class, and they will marvel as they learn. This means that you will need to find out what will motivate this group. "Instead of imposing reasons for valuing learning on students, educators can help them make the connections between their lives and what they are learning." (Hulleman & Hulleman, 2018).

When your classroom has motivated students, the content will flow more easily; they will participate in the lessons and pay attention to what is being said. They will desire to learn and absorb what is being said. By motivating students, you will be helping them be more resilient and self-assured, increasing their academic self-esteem, which can later impact other areas of their lives. You will also see new talent develop and creative minds at work. It will allow them to learn critical thinking skills and persist with academic tasks.

But sometimes, some issues cannot be solved with motivation alone. As we will see in the next section, some problems may require other kinds of intervention. Let's look at some examples and talk more about them and how they can affect your classroom.

WHEN MOTIVATION IS NOT ENOUGH

We all have basic needs. That is, there is a certain degree of wellness required to carry out daily tasks. We must be well rested, fed, and feel some sense of security. No teacher can take it for granted that their students come from a safe and secure environment. Any student can come from a home that is socially or financially insecure. Their households may lack basic necessities like electricity, running water, food, or consistent shelter.

As educators, we must recognize that all students may not come from a supportive or nurturing home—and even if their immediate family is a safe one, the neighborhood outside their home may not be. Some students face the challenges of gangs, drugs, or job insecurity, making internal or external motivation hard to find in their lives. We cannot always change the adverse circumstances that students face outside the school. What we can do, however, is acknowledge these obstacles and provide them with tools and strategies to reach their full potential despite them. Let's work together to empower our students and create a brighter future. Imagine a world where all students have the opportunity to thrive. With our help, we can make it a reality.

Apart from the toxic situations that students might come from, we also must consider that we live in a globalized world, where people from different cultures blend in with our own. This means that immigrants who barely speak English attend schools unprepared to help them with ESL programs—simply because no one knows their mother tongue. Is it their fault? Of course not! Children and teenagers have the **right** to learn. However, we need a structure to provide them with the best aid possible. We need these students to marvel at the opportunities they will find.

I can bet that if you look at the most unmotivated students in your classroom with analytical eyes, you can find some who fit these descriptions. The question now is, *How can I help?* In some cases, it is essential to include the student's parents and the school administration. Sometimes, this might even help you gain a more complete understanding of a student's academic history or home environment.

On the other hand, there will be times when the responsibility to intervene will fall solely on your shoulders. Parents may already be stretched to their limits; administrators may be uncooperative, or perhaps their attention and resources are necessarily directed elsewhere. You become the last line of defense for your student. And you know what? Even if you **think** you cannot do it, I can assure you, you can. You **are** a teacher. You **are** a role model. You **can** be a motivator for students. And, of course, you **are able** to find creative solutions. Remember the marvelous professional that you are! No matter how overwhelmed you may be, I know for a fact that this motivation for helping your students is within you. Furthermore, I think helping them will probably help you **reduce** your daily stress with a more cooperative classroom.

Use your intuition! You have it, and it is your ally! "When we act with the guidance of our intuition, then we no longer need to feel motivated or find motivation. We feel inspired. Inspired action comes from within." (Lattimer, 2020).

UNLEASHING STUDENT MOTIVATION FOR MARVELOUS LEARNING

Ana, a recent immigrant from Guatemala, was sixteen years old and found adapting to her new life in New York City challenging. She needed more motivation in class, frequently missed sessions, and showed little interest in her studies. Although her classmates assured me she attended school regularly, she remained unresponsive to their attempts to involve her in class. As her Spanish literature teacher, I noticed her lack of participation and felt inspired to reach out to her.

One day, I spoke with Ana after class and discovered she missed her family, particularly her grandmother, back in Guatemala. I listened to her stories about her life before coming to the USA, and it made a difference that someone cared about her. Rather than pressure her to perform better in class, I offered her articles on successful Latin American immigrants and encouraged her to continue working hard.

Gradually, Ana began to transform. She began to participate more in class, raising her hand to answer questions, and even initiated conversations with her classmates, making friends along the way. In her senior year, she wrote a heartfelt letter thanking all her teachers for their encouragement and support, stating that she had gone from being an unmotivated student to one determined to succeed. She credited her teachers for believing in her when she could not believe in herself.

As teachers, we have the power to inspire and uplift our students. We can empower them to overcome challenges and achieve their dreams by listening and showing genuine care. Remember that every student is unique, with their own story, and it is our responsibility to support and guide them toward their fullest potential. Together, we can make a positive difference in the lives of our students and help them realize their true potential.

AWAKENING YOUR TEACHER GENIUS: THE MARVELOUS ACT OF SELF-MOTIVATION

Here are some tips for connecting with your own motivation and creating a more productive classroom:

- **Keep your purposes clear:** It's essential to be clear on your reasons for teaching. Write them down somewhere you can see and easily access them if needed. Read it and remind yourself of the reasons you do what you do.
- **Breathe:** Think about colors as you inhale and exhale. The color you inhale should be the color of what you feel, and the color you exhale that of what you want to feel.
- **Feel your body:** Be sure you are aware of your full body and conscious of your movements.
- **Stop, look, and listen:** Look around and see what is happening. Take a moment to reflect on your surroundings. Hear the sounds and be aware of your environment.
- **Write in a journal:** When you let your feelings go and write openly about the problems you face in the

classroom, it may help you see things more clearly. Be sure you are open and honest so that your creative mind works fully.

3

FROM PURPOSELESSNESS TO PURPOSEFULNESS: CULTIVATING MEANING

> "The great aim of education is not knowledge but action."
>
> — HERBERT SPENCER

If you've ever found yourself uttering the words, "What's the point of it all?" then you know how crucial it is to discover purpose and meaning in life. For some, the search for that meaning can be lifelong. But it's not just adults who need to find their purpose; it's also essential for the students in your classroom. Two decades ago, the focus was primarily on well-being and being a good person. Now, thanks to the contributions of modern-day philosophers, we understand that discovering meaning is equally important. According to Thaddeus Metz (2021), there's a wealth of literature on life's purpose, reflecting how vibrant this field has become.

In this chapter, we'll explore how teachers can play a pivotal role in helping their students find purpose and meaning in their lives. I'll show you how guiding your students toward a goal and helping them establish lifelong aspirations can be magical. Remember that some students may come from complex backgrounds and face more challenges than others. However, as we teach them to ask the right questions, we give them the tools to establish their purpose and see life's endless possibilities. So, let's take that first step together: By asking questions, we can help our students discover the beauty of their existence.

EMPOWERING THROUGH THE ART OF QUESTIONING

Questions are a powerful tool in the classroom, yet sometimes we forget their impact. Have you ever overlooked a hand going up, feeling too tired or overwhelmed to answer? This is a missed opportunity to help your students thrive. But don't worry: There's a solution! By embracing the power of questions, you can create an environment that inspires and motivates your students. Imagine a classroom where every student feels seen and heard and where you, as a teacher, feel confident and in control. This kind of classroom can change lives, and it all starts with the simple act of asking and answering questions. Let's prioritize questions in our teaching practice and show our students that their questions matter! Let's create a culture of curiosity where every question is welcomed and celebrated. With this mindset, we can transform our classrooms from dull and routine to vibrant and inspiring.

The point here is not to tell you what you should or should not do, but rather ask you to consider other options. Let's try not to look at the student as if they are "disturbing" the class. Have you considered how **positive** it is that they are actually asking questions? This is because when they do, they are **showing interest** and **learning**.

When you consider the number of things involved in asking questions, remember that it is a complex process involving several steps. When students ask a question, they have thought about what they want to know, formed the question in their mind, and finally, verbalized it to the teacher (*Why Is Asking and Answering Questions Important?*, 2018). The process unfolds when you ask them a question: They access their minds to find the answer among the content they have learned, think about what the question means, understand it, elaborate an answer, and finally, speak up.

Did you know your brain can change and grow as you use it? It's called neuroplasticity. By practicing a specific thinking pattern, your brain becomes wired to follow that pattern in the future. If you need help with classroom management or feel unmotivated, don't worry. With the power of neuroplasticity, you can become the master teacher you were meant to be. By consistently practicing and repeating new skills, you can wire your brain to become more skilled at managing your classroom and inspiring your students. Embrace the power of neuroplasticity and unlock your potential as a teacher!

Dear teacher, you are vital to your students' growth and development. To help them succeed, it's important to use analogies and encourage questions. Why? Because every time your students ask a question, they build new pathways in their brains that allow them to better understand and remember the information you're sharing. This is all thanks to neuroplasticity, the remarkable ability of the brain to change and adapt with use. By tapping into this feature, you can unlock your full potential as a teacher and empower your students to reach new heights of learning.

Kelley Spainhour states that a few techniques related to the subject can be used to help students enhance their learning in the classroom. These include:

- Repetition of the content by applying it in several contexts.
- Use of the student's prior knowledge and association techniques.
- Incorporation of movement into the content being taught.
- Offering challenges that are adequate to their learning age.

In addition, I would also add the most important one: **Enable students to ask questions**. To further illustrate its importance, I want you to take a moment and return to a particular time. Revisit a time when you were in school, in a similar place to where your students are now. Think about these questions:

- *Did I learn better when I asked questions?*
- *How did I feel when my questions were answered?*

- *How did I feel when my questions were not answered?*
- *Did asking questions help me be more engaged in the classroom?*

Your answers might be similar to those of any other person I ask. *Yes, I found it easier to learn when I could ask questions,* and *Yes, asking questions helped me be more engaged in the class.* At the same time, *I had a good feeling when I was allowed to ask questions, and the teacher answered them,* and *I felt discouraged and demotivated when this was impossible.*

When students are curious about something, it can also help trigger a hormonal reaction in which dopamine is released into the brain, and they feel instant **gratification** (Riddell & McDermott, 2014). On the other hand, if a student fears asking a question because they fear being humiliated or reprimanded, they might lose this rewarding opportunity. Have you ever seen the face of a student who asked a question, and your answer was, "Wow, that is a really good question!"? This is because they are being rewarded for asking, and dopamine is acting in their bodies.

Therefore, we need to enable our students to practice the extraordinary ability of asking questions. Changing your perspective and approach to dialogue in the classroom may also alter your lessons and your own level of motivation. Realize that when students ask questions, they learn and engage with your class, showing interest. And what more do we want as teachers?

If that is not enough, in addition, think about the fact that when students ask questions, they are also helping **you** become a better professional. Yes, that's right. Just like their brain is working when they are asking or answering a question, the same will happen to you. You might need to find a new way to answer something they do not understand, or search for alternatives that make sense to them. Have you ever thought about this?

And why is all of this important? Well, because by enabling your students to ask questions, no matter what they are, you are enabling them to find the **meaning** of things. Whether this is about how they will learn the content or take it into a deeper context, asking questions will "train" their brains to do the same in other situations. And this, in some time, will be the beginning of their journey of identifying and relating to a **purpose**.

THE NEED FOR PURPOSE

Consider a small child and their boundless curiosity. They constantly ask questions about what things are for and how they can be used. This is because a young age, we marvel at things and are fascinated by the world and how everything works. As we age, we lose that sense of wonder and purpose. We go through the motions, needing more direction and meaning. But the need for purpose is innate in us all. It motivates us to learn, grow, and contribute to the world around us.

As we grow, however, our interest can slowly fade if no one answers our questions or encourages us to ask them in the first place. Even when we excel at searching the Internet, for example, we may end up wasting our time and gain unsatisfactory results if we do not know **what** and **how** to ask. Little by little, our interest in these subjects will diminish. What is worse, so will our sense of **purpose**. And why is this important? Before answering, let me ask you something: Have you ever seen someone **without** a purpose?

Individuals who do not have a purpose are "more vulnerable to boredom, anxiety, and depression." (Taylor, 2013). In addition, they are more prone to addictive behavior with drugs and alcohol, for example, and negative feelings. Remember a situation in which you have seen a person without a purpose. What were their actions like? How did they react and respond to life? Were they good role models?

When talking about students in our classroom, those without a purpose are some of the easiest to spot. They do not care for what they are learning and seem to be there just because someone is "making them." These youngsters do not have something to look forward to, a reason to do what they do, and are usually the ones who will shrug off any comment you might make to help engage or motivate them. You will see that these are the most disengaged from the lesson, homework, and other activities. This makes them disruptive, and they will generally not listen to you in class.

As teachers, it's our responsibility to help our students find purpose and understand the relevance of school for their future. While we may get an occasional, "Why do I need to learn this?" question, we must strive to give meaningful answers that inspire and motivate our students. It's easy to provide automatic responses to maintain order, but we must remember the importance of sparking curiosity and passion in our students. With purpose comes engagement, and with engagement comes a harmonious and productive classroom environment.

However, what if we looked at this from another perspective and helped the students to realize the direct impact the content has on their future? All of your students will not become rocket scientists, but we must be able to show them the purpose of what they are learning for the present moment by incorporating it into their lives. "Teachers around the country are discovering that these types of real-world projects provide the perfect foundation to naturally integrate content understanding." (Tarango, 2019).

Motivated students will be more participative in class and **willing** to engage, learn, and cooperate. Creating projects that take them away from the "textbook" approach of the classroom is one of the ways this can be done. If you want to have even more success, you might want to try to identify what they like and their hobbies, for example, and how you can adjust these with the lessons you teach. And this can be done independently if you teach math, science, history, or biology. You can **always** find something that they can relate to. How often have I seen students marvel at how associations of their interests could be done with the content I was teaching?

By allowing them to reflect on what they want to do or who they want to be, you will be helping them establish a sense of purpose and possibly **enjoy** the lesson you give. Help them establish SMART goals, those that are specific, measurable, achievable, realistic and timely. Aid them in determining what their purpose is **now**. What are their goals, dreams, and objectives? Finally, help them see, through challenging them, that they **are** capable and that it **is** possible. Once they find their identity, what makes them unique and special, you will see them grow and evolve—all because they have found themselves and can now determine their purpose.

AUTHENTIC IDENTITY

Have you ever asked someone why they chose their profession, only to receive a range of answers? Did it align with your personal values and passions, or was there a particular subject in school that inspired you? Perhaps a doctor enjoyed science in school, while a journalist found their love of reading and writing in English classes. Reflecting on your motivations for choosing this career is essential as a teacher. By understanding how your educational experiences helped shape your authentic identity, you can better connect with your students and help them do the same.

One of the wonders of the educational environment is that it enables students to find purpose in their lives or, more specifically, what they want to do with their future. This is important because, according to Steger et al. (2021), "There is a gap between what young people want and what we appear to offer them as a society." And this is where the school comes in. Several schools have established programs within their curricula to help students find the meaning of their life through guidance sessions and special programs. I dare you to guess who are the professionals who are most involved in this process. If you said "teachers," then you are correct!

"Across these meaning-focused programs, the experimental groups reported higher meaning in life, a clearer sense of career direction, more insight into themselves, and better preparedness for the future." Steger et al. (2021). This is because identity is one of the foundations of education, and is necessary for students to understand who they are and their role in the world. As toddlers become children and then teenagers, the importance of school in their lives increases, making it an essential step in developing their character and future. How astonishing is this?

As these students evolve, it will be possible to start seeing traits of their personality and topics that spike their interest. They become more skilled in identifying what they like and what they can easily relate to. Hence, they choose what they want to do and be in their future, leading them to understand life's larger and more general truths. This recognition will be the baseline to help them relate to others, communicate, and establish social relationships around them. Kuurme and Carlsson (2012) state, "Learning, as a process that accompanies human growth and occurs throughout life, plays a central role in identity formation and can be consciously directed."

The main reason for this is that when an individual is looking to find their authentic identity, they will look for meaning and purpose and how these can apply to their lives. Especially during this phase of their lives, they will start questioning themselves on matters such as *What do I want to be? What is my purpose in this world? How do I fit in the context into which I am inserted? Where do I belong?* All these reflections will deeply impact how they perceive and react to the learning process in school.

Students who do not see the advantage of learning something because they cannot **relate** to it will not pay attention in class, and might become disruptive and confrontational. The level of attention they pay to your class will depend on whether they find it useful, significant, and important to them and to the goals they have established for their lives. However, this does not mean that a student who wants to become a doctor would not be interested in history.

It is all a matter of approach. They might not be interested in how the continents were separated in the Pangaea, but they may be interested in how primitive people practiced medicine and the technology they used. The approach given to the subject will depend on the teacher, so that the needs of all the different personalities and authentic individualities of the students are addressed in class. For example, you might be teaching them about Ancient Greece and, to ensure that they are interested, request a research project related to the area that interests them the most—philosophy, biology, chemistry, or astronomy. This way, students will be learning and identifying with the subject simultaneously.

In the study published by Kuurme and Carlsson (2012), they claim that there is

Perceived contradiction between the realities of organizationally defined learning and the ideals contained in the associated learning for identity concepts. The subsequent discourse reveals the possibility that schools alienate young learners from authentic learning. According to critics, school ignores students' prior experience, focuses on standardized achievement, narrows content to a few chosen texts, excludes social and emotional substance, maintains a stifling status quo, places learning on a competitive basis, and precludes deep relations between a learner and the content as learning is metered out in consumptive fashion (section 4, para. 1, *The Probability of Authenticity Experiences in School-based Learning*).

This means that **we** need to be the change. **We**, as teachers, must help these students find their authentic selves through how and what we teach. Most of the time, school lessons are so standard that they do not take into consideration the cultural difference of our students, for example. It is **up to us** to make this change and to give them significance—especially if their conditions outside the school are unfavorable. How can a student think about the future if they come from a toxic environment? How can they learn the basics of what they need to know if they cannot concentrate? To answer this, we must ask ourselves, *How can I, as a teacher, help my students learn what is important in life?* We must think about **our purpose** for teaching and not merely the content we teach.

What Is Important to Learn in Life?

One of the most important things that we can learn in this life is **who we are**. This includes knowing what we like, what we don't like, what is important to us and what is irrelevant, what motivates us, and what makes us feel down. Knowing more about ourselves is essential to taking the first step to finding out meaning and purpose. If you do not like the sight of blood, you might not want to become a doctor. If you feel too shy, maybe being a teacher is not the best professional path.

If you consider that school is one of the first social environments we must navigate, it is also the place where we learn some of the most important things in life. The first, and one of the most important, is how to interact with others. We learn how to interact with people from different cultures, diverse economic statuses, and various backgrounds. We are given the tools to learn how to communicate with them through group activities, projects, and interactions between breaks.

I also don't think I need to mention that school is responsible for teaching students skills and strategies they will carry for life. It all depends on their interaction with the environment and how they perceive their learning process. "Just as there may be natural affinities among the dimensions of meaning and certain academic content areas, there is a great deal of freedom and creativity with which these connections can be made. The connections simply need to be translated and elaborated." (Steger et al., 2021).

Social studies can help them understand various cultures and their differences. **Music** and **art** help stimulate creativity. **Math** and **physics** stimulate logical thinking and problem-solving skills. **Biology** and **chemistry** help us determine the impact we have on the world. **History** aids in learning how what we do impacts the larger picture of our context. And finally, **literature**, **languages**, and **writing** help us communicate with others and understand the subtleties of communication between individuals.

Once students identify these possibilities, relating what they are learning in school to their life **outside** school, they will start to see the importance of education. But they cannot do this alone. They are not trained for this—**we are**. They lack maturity and are still in their learning process. As teachers, it is up to us to help them see the advantages of education and absorb the most benefits from the situation. It is, therefore, our job to create a sense of awe and help them see the importance of the school environment in building character and identifying their authentic self.

UNLEASHING THE SECRETS TO STUDENTS' AUTHENTICITY: THE MARVELOUS PATH TO SELF-DISCOVERY

Dear fellow teachers, let me share a powerful story that inspired me to connect with my students and reignite my passion for teaching. I faced a challenging situation in the South Bronx when my students were disengaged, disrespectful, and completely uninterested in learning. I felt powerless and unmotivated, but I knew I had to find a way to inspire them.

I witnessed a remarkable transformation in my students by creating a game that led them to share their hobbies, passions, and desired knowledge. They gained ownership of their education and became more enthusiastic about attending class. Even the most notorious class skippers showed up eagerly for their Spanish literature class! That's when I discovered the power of letting students take control of their education.

As my students started to learn more about their interests, they found meaning in their lives, and their views on how the classroom could be shifted. They were eager to share what they had learned with others and inspire their peers. Witnessing their transformation was truly rewarding as a teacher.

I learned that the best way to teach is to let your students lead. By doing so, not only did I inspire my students, but I also inspired myself. Whenever I face a challenging class, I remind myself there's always a way to connect with my students and encourage them to find meaning in what they do in the classroom. This approach is a powerful way to inspire your students and begin finding meaning in your life.

I have another story to share with you. It's about a student named Miguel, who was known as one of the most unruly kids in school. One teacher decided to take a different approach, and it changed everything.

Instead of punishing or scolding Miguel, this teacher tried to understand him. She gave him more attention, greeted him daily, and even asked him about his interests and hobbies. She noticed he had a drawing talent, so she encouraged him to bring his artwork to class. Slowly but surely, Miguel began to open up.

In direct response to the attention and respect he received from his teacher, Miguel's attendance, punctuality, and level of engagement all improved dramatically. He began coming to class on time every day, and he became an active participant of class discussions. Nonetheless, there were still times when he would act out or disrupt the class. Instead of getting angry or frustrated, the teacher would take a deep breath and remind herself that he was still learning to express himself healthily. Even when students show improvement, she knew that growth doesn't happen overnight. That's one of the unavoidable truths of dealing with youth.

And while it wasn't automatic, Miguel did mature in his communication style over time. He used his artwork as a tool to help him express his emotions, and it worked wonders. He even handed his teacher a drawing he had made of a tree, representing his growth and progress. That tree is a powerful metaphor for the possibilities you can unlock in students. A tree grows from the smallest of seeds and takes many years to mature. At the same time, when it is nurtured and allowed to grow deep roots, it becomes one of the strongest and most enduring life forms in the natural world. In fact, a well-rooted tree becomes a source of life for countless other forms of life around it. The same can be true of students in the classroom in the ways their personalities motivate others. And the same is true of you.

This teacher's approach helped Miguel find a way to express himself healthily and positively. From that day forward, Miguel continued to make progress. He still had moments of defiance and rebellion, but this teacher had earned his trust and respect. He even started helping other struggling students, showing them the same kindness and understanding he had been shown. In this way, the time that Miguel's teacher took to nurture him had a positive ripple effect throughout the school community.

This story reminds us of the power of empathy and understanding in education. Even the most unruly students can be transformed with the right approach. Ultimately, they want to connect, be loved, accepted, and understood. So let us take this lesson to heart and strive to create a safe and welcoming learning environment for all our students.

Turn your classroom into a nucleus of dynamic ideas, inspiring stories, and unbreakable connections.

"Teaching is the highest form of understanding."

— ARISTOTLE

In the introduction to this book, I stressed the importance of finding meaning, inspiration, and purpose in your own journey, in order to create an enlightened learning environment for your students.

By finding new, personalized ways to motivate your students and helping them discover their most authentic selves, you will see teaching in a more meaningful light. There is nothing more inspiring as a teacher than igniting the spark of change in your students. Helping them find their passion fuels your own.

By now, you will have seen that there is no "one-size-fits-all solution" to unleashing your students' full potential. What works for one student won't necessarily work for the next.

Some need someone to listen to them, others are desperately looking for a role to fulfill. Yet others have great expectations for their own life… but they need someone to illuminate the way ahead.

You probably never expected teaching to be this way. At college, you were taught how to create course content, time your classes, and grade exams and essays.

Education's true essence lies within oneself, where the desire to impact students' lives profoundly drives educators to adopt diverse strategies, potentially creating a transformative experience for struggling learners. If you found value in this insight, as a fellow teacher, I request your support in spreading this knowledge among educators worldwide.

A few minutes of your time can revolutionize teaching with dynamic, creative approaches, impacting educators significantly.

By leaving a review of this book on Amazon, you'll show other educators that the best way to teach is to let their students lead.

Please spread the word about this book's impact, guiding teachers to transform their classes into student highlights.

Thank you so much for your help. By being the best teacher you can be, you can help students unleash their full potential.

Scan the QR code below

4

THE MYTHIC MARVEL: EMPOWERING EDUCATION THROUGH STORYTELLING

> *"We're so engaged in doing things to achieve purposes of outer value that we forget the inner value, the rapture that is associated with being alive, is what it is all about."*
>
> — JOSEPH CAMPBELL

Do you remember the myths that you were taught from your own school days? Those stories from ancient Egypt, Greece, Rome, China, and beyond that still resonate with us today. They were more than just fables. They were transformative tales that could spark a sense of awe and wonder in us all. Using myths in the classroom is one of the most empowering techniques available to teachers.

Some may think that myths have no real value in the twenty-first century. This is a misconception. Myths offer timeless wisdom and insights that remain relevant today, conveyed through fantastic or fictitious narratives that inspire awe and convey universal truths. Ancient and modern myths are metaphors that can be decoded or interpreted to reveal their deeper meanings. Unfortunately, our educational system has largely overlooked the power of myths. Greek and Latin, along with their mythologies, were pushed out of schools, leaving only a few famous names for children to memorize. It's time to recognize the incredible educational potential of these stories.

So what exactly is a myth? It's a story that often features a hero, gods, or supernatural beings that helps explain the unexplainable. They're full of mystical or fantastical elements that leave us with a sense of awe and wonder. They were used for centuries to impart wisdom and moral lessons to listeners. Think about the ancient Egyptians, who used the story of the sun god Ra to explain why the sun rises and sets every day.

As we will see further in this chapter, myths have four essential functions, according to historian and mythologist Joseph Campbell. These functions are significant to student learning. Myths provide students with something that cannot be replicated through traditional educational subjects like math, language arts, science or history. Myths provide the experience of the wonderful, the unexplainable, and the mysterious. In a mysterious cosmos, myth is the attempt to explain the unexplainable through metaphors, leaving us with a sense of astonishment that keeps our mind awake with the desire to seek more answers in life. Learning through myths and storytelling is an opportunity to engage and empower our students, providing them with a sense of awe and wonder, opening doors to the unexplored realms of the mind, and allowing them to tap into the full extent of their potential. By the end of this chapter, you will understand how to use myths and storytelling to transform your classroom and empower your students to reach new heights of learning and growth.

MY UNDERSTANDING OF MYTHS

Besides explaining reality through metaphorical stories in which gods, heroes, and legendary entities are the protagonists, myths always express universal truths. Myths also provide images and symbols that touch aspects of our subconscious mind, factors that are unreachable through purely rational examination. That's why myths are timeless and so powerful.

Our fascination with myths is evident in the captivating tales that have endured over time. Take, for example, the story of Aphrodite, who emerged from the sea foam, or the legend of Lord Hanuman, a giant god-monkey who—as narrated in the Rāmāyaṇa—flew from India to Sri Lanka with a mountain in his hand to rescue Princess Sita. There's the story of Zeus, who, smitten with Princess Danaë, transformed into a "shower of gold" to enter her chamber and, without sexual intercourse, made her pregnant with the demigod Perseus. These are just a few examples of the great myths and legends that continue to captivate and inspire us, despite their fantastical nature.

People often get caught up in the "historical accuracy" of myths. But it's important to remember that myths aren't meant to be taken as literal history. They are metaphorical, sublime, and complex poetry that allude to universal and eternal truths.

Myths express timeless wisdom and remind us of our humanity by acknowledging the limitations of our understanding of the world and our own minds. They invite us to embrace the unknown and recognize that there are aspects of our consciousness that we may never fully comprehend.

Moreover, ancient myths have profound educational value. They offer insights into how our ancestors understood the world, which also helps us understand our present. While myths incentivize our imagination, they also inform us about critical societal matters. Through their narratives, myths provide perspectives on violence, politics, misogyny, murder, slavery, and human rights, among other topics. By exploring these themes within the mythological framework, we gain a deeper understanding of our human condition and the historical context in which these myths originated. In this way, myths serve as both poetic expressions and educational tools. They transcend time, offering a glimpse into our past while guiding us to reflect on our present and future.

Myths also invite us to recognize our humanity. They remind us that we do not understand some aspects of our mind and that our consciousness is limited. The story of Achilles' heel is one of the myths that captures this idea perfectly. As a baby, Achilles was immersed in a sacred fountain by his mother, Thetis, which made him invincible to any weapon. But when she held him upside down, she forgot to submerge his heels, leaving them vulnerable. Achilles' heel became his only weak spot, ultimately leading to his downfall. Despite his legendary strength and skill as a warrior, he was slain by a single arrow shot by Paris, a weak and inexperienced fighter who lacked the abilities of his brother Hector. Ironically, such a small oversight could bring down such a powerful hero, and only a few gods knew of his vulnerability.

The myth of Achilles' heel can be interpreted in many ways, but one common theme is that humans may not always see or understand things fully. This notion is analogous to the yin-yang symbol in Chinese philosophy, where the white point in the black half represents things beyond our understanding, and the black point in the white half represents the same. Achilles' heel myth invites us to consider the possibility of hidden vulnerabilities, things that, in ourselves or others, may be overlooked or underestimated. Despite his invincibility, Achilles had a fatal flaw that ultimately led to his downfall. Similarly, we may have blind spots that could have consequences if left unaddressed. The myth also serves as a cautionary tale and a reminder of the importance of humility and self-awareness.

FOUR FUNCTIONS OF MYTHS

As I mentioned earlier, the importance of myth cannot be overrated. They help us have a deeper understanding of something, insights that otherwise we would not have if not for the attempt that it provides. We can say, "Myths are the stories we tell that define us. The truth of myth doesn't lie in its historicity, its historical accuracy, but in what it expresses about what we believe." (Stifler, n.d.). Myth has served several purposes, and according to Joseph Campbell's interview with Bill Moyers, published by the Joseph Campbell Foundation (2022), myths serve four main purposes, which we will examine in this section.

The Mystical Purpose

Do you ever feel lost or uncertain in your life? Do you struggle to find meaning or purpose? According to mythologist Joseph Campbell, myths can help us connect with a more profound sense of meaning and purpose. He refers to this as "the mystical purpose" of myths. By exploring the stories and symbols of myths, we can tap into universal truths and connect with something greater than ourselves. This can give us a sense of direction and help us navigate the challenges and uncertainties of life. So if you're feeling lost or need inspiration, consider exploring the myths and legends that have captivated and inspired people for generations.

Mythologies from various cultures, including Egyptian, Indian, and Greek, contain numerous stories suggesting a higher power or force that exists beyond the dimensions of human understanding. This belief is reflected not only in the mythological tales themselves but also in the characters' hierarchical structure. For example, in Greek mythology, even the most powerful gods, such as Zeus, are subject to something greater than themselves. Zeus is bound by the three Moirai or Fates, goddesses who ensure that every being, mortal and divine, lives out their destiny as assigned by the laws of the universe. While this is just one example, other mythological narrations depict a similar notion of a divine force that governs the world. By exploring these mythological tales and the hierarchy of the characters within them, we can gain a deeper understanding of the belief in a higher power that has existed throughout human history.

The Greeks used myths like this one, and countless others across different cultures, to explain things and make sense of the real world, or life, by connecting it with the human soul and its essence. Essentially, myths help us to honor fundamental change and insurmountable impermanence while allowing us to make sense of being or not being in a universe that has no meaning other than the meaning we bring to it (McGee, 2018). By exploring myths and their mystical purpose, we can learn more about ourselves and our place in the world, and find more profound meaning and purpose in life.

The Cosmological Purpose

The second purpose of the myth, according to Campbell, is **cosmological**. Although it might be similar to the mythical concept, it has a different approach since it will talk about how early societies made sense of why things happened in the world. You can think of cosmology as a way to bring a sense of order to phenomena that are difficult to understand (such as the beginning of the universe) with the tools of inquiry we have available. Myths serve a cosmological purpose because they offer explanations that help bring comfort to those who hear them. Without myths, people can become overwhelmed by the unknown in a negative way rather than a positive way. They may experience anxiety, fear, or confusion rather than a sense of reverence, curiosity, or awe. According to Drury (2019), when the world is chaotic, "We look for those who can restore order, those who seem to make it all make sense with their wisdom and sometimes, by sheer force of will. To be mythic is to restore order."

While modern science has given us a more precise understanding of the natural world, exploring mythological tales' different layers and interpretation levels can still offer meaning and insight. The ancient Greeks used the myth of Demeter and Persephone to explain soil fertility and the changing seasons. The presence of Persephone with her mother determined whether the land would thrive, and when she was with her husband, Hades, the land would not produce anything because Demeter was sad. The story of Demeter and Persephone may not help us understand weather conditions in the twenty-first century. Still, it can teach us about mother-daughter relationships and offer us a framework for understanding our experiences in the world.

Myths have been a way for cultures to explain their beliefs and understand the world around them. Hindu mythology, for example, tells the story of Brahma creating the world from a piece of himself and creating all the creatures, gods, demons, good and bad, light and darkness. This creation myth, in its own way, is analogous to those found in other cultures, such as the Genesis account for Christians and Jews and the remains of the giant Ymir told in the legends of the Vikings. These myths may have tried to explain the world's origin before the scientific theory of the Big Bang. Nevertheless, they still offer insight into the values and beliefs of each culture. We can learn about humanity's shared experiences and unique perspectives by exploring the similarities and differences in creation myths.

The Sociological Purpose

In the quest for personal growth and fulfillment, we often overlook the profound sociological purpose of myths. As Campbell observed, myths play a crucial role in maintaining social order and reinforcing cultural values within a community. They are a powerful tool for transmitting norms, beliefs, and customs from one generation to another, creating a shared framework of understanding and meaning that unites and strengthens society. By featuring archetypal characters and universal themes that resonate across cultures, myths foster a sense of commonality and shared experience, inspiring individuals to adopt desirable behaviors and values. In short, myths contribute to building and preserving a cohesive and functional society, offering us a blueprint for living in harmony with ourselves and others.

Myths have been integral to human societies since ancient times, not only as entertainment, but as a means of establishing social norms and moral codes. According to Campbell, traditional communities relied on myths as the essential building blocks of ethical conduct, using them to bind people together and reinforce shared values and beliefs. Even today, the influence of myths can be seen in our actions, especially in religions that use stories to guide behavior. By reconnecting with the wisdom of myths, we can tap into a timeless source of guidance and inspiration, enriching our lives and relationships with others.

One of the myths' most potent sociological functions is to provide a Sacred Center for people. This Center could be physical or spiritual. The main temple or sanctuary, typically in the city center, served as the area's tallest and most important building, referring people to the eternal Reality that corresponds to the Center. For instance, when a Muslim person in Damascus or a Catholic in Florence went to the temple, it was believed that their movement was a ritual in which the believer metaphorically dramatized their inner search for their optimal journey to Paradise. Going to the main temple—an activity commonly found in myth or legend—was a way of allegorically recreating the human soul's journey to the Divine, inspiring the believer to embark on an inner quest for self-discovery and transcendence. By joining with other community members on this journey, the temple, sanctuary, or holy city offered a sense of belonging and connection to something greater than oneself. Whether we seek to connect with the divine or each other, the notion of a Sacred Center reminds us of the power of community and the importance of shared purpose in our personal and social development.

The Pedagogical Purpose of Myths

According to Campbell, the pedagogical purpose of myths is the most important one. Myths tackle unchanging human themes like love, revenge, mortality, immortality, and more. They are powerful tools for teaching people about life, meaning, and navigating certain situations. For instance, the story of Odysseus teaches the importance of perseverance and warns against pride, while King Arthur's legend emphasizes the value of honor, chivalry, and loyalty. Additionally, myths are crucial for transmitting cultural values and traditions across generations, conveying moral lessons, and preserving cultural identities. In summary, myths offer valuable insights into the complexities of life, inspiring us to live more meaningful and fulfilling lives.

If you think about how most myths are told, there is usually a situation in which there is a problem, a trigger moment in which the main character realizes something. He carries out a certain action (or fights evil or the problem), and the issue is resolved. When you look at a myth from this point of view, it is teaching people how they should conduct their lives and what they should do when they are faced with a situation in which they do not know how to act. This means that "Myths, at their heart, aren't about gods, or monsters, or whatever, but about human beings; and that if we observe a myth closely, we'll discover clues on how we can live." (Drury, 2020).

Myths and stories play a crucial role in learning and teaching. Sometimes, the most effective way to communicate the truth or solve a problem is by telling a relatable story. We can see this approach in the Bible, where Jesus taught his disciples through parables, and in epic poems like the Mahābhārata, the Iliad, and the Odyssey, which were transmitted orally for hundreds of years before being written down. Without the power of storytelling, these stories would have been recovered to the sands of time. By incorporating elements of surprise, adventure, humor, or love, accounts can capture the listener's attention and engage them in the narrative. Ultimately, myths and stories are powerful tools for conveying essential knowledge and preserving cultural traditions across generations.

Myths in education can be a vital tool for teachers to connect with their students, and as an essential method to enhance teaching techniques. By using metaphors, teachers can help students understand the meaning behind a lesson and support the content being taught. In this case, the myths will "help us understand and contextualize our experiences. Further, myth allows us to encounter the offerings in ways that are aesthetically powerful and that remind us of our own human gift of creative response" (Goldstein, 2003).

Let's talk about one of these potential myths—the Greek tale of the wings of Icarus. In this story, a mythical inventor called Daedalus and his son Icarus were prisoners on the island of Crete and wanted to escape. To do this, Daedalus created a pair of wings that were made of feathers and wax. Because of this, the wings were sensitive to heat. Icarus put on his wings to escape, and despite his father's warnings not to fly too close to the sun, he still did it, which led to the melting of the wax. As a result, the wings fell apart, and Icarus fell from the sky into the water, meeting his death.

Teachers can create awe-inspiring moments that engage students and leave a lasting impression by weaving myths into lessons. The ancient Greek myth of Icarus, who flew too close to the sun and perished as a result, has given rise to the cautionary expression "We should not fly too close to the sun," which warns us against taking excessive risks or overreaching in our pursuits. Additionally, the story advises young people to listen to their parents, as their advice is rooted in experience and love. Including myths like this in educational instructions can work wonders in students' learning processes. They help teachers establish a deeper connection between students and the subject matter, enabling students to learn essential life lessons.

This is why myths were, and still are, so crucial in the classroom and throughout the teaching process. As we will now see, our students start to develop their personal identities through the use of myth since "using the arts allows them to tap easily into two powerful sources of wisdom and knowledge" (Goldstein, 2003).

TEENS DEVELOP THEIR IDENTITIES THROUGH PERSONAL MYTH

When we think that children and teenagers develop their personalities during the phase in which they attend school, it is essential to understand the role that the education system will have in their identity development. Scholars understand that the processes they undergo in school will be an important marker for understanding how they see and relate to life, because of the psychological process they undergo during this phase. To better understand this concept, there is a line of study in psychology called narrative development, which states that humans create identities through constructing narratives and stories about their lives, and by listening to and observing others as they develop (McAdams & McLean, 2013).

"The idea is that via the process of narrating their experiences, people eventually build a sense of how their past informs the person they are today and how both their past and present point toward an emerging future" (Mclean & Pasupathi, 2010). This means that teens will not only develop their identities through the stories that they listen to but also through the process that they create. In this sense, we must understand that it is essential to allow our students to learn how to create their own personal myths based on their experiences and life events, to help them make sense of life and the things they have lived through.

In a quote that Chen (2018) extracts from the psychologist Dan McAdams' book *The Stories We Live By: Personal Myths and the Making of the Self*, she states, "We do not discover ourselves through myth, we make ourselves through myth." If you consider the classic example of children playing the "telephone game" to convey a message, this is easy to understand. In this case, you line up the students in your class and whisper to the first one a phrase. As the message is being transmitted from person to person, each one will develop their own understanding of what is being said, and when the final student needs to state the message they understood out loud, you will see that it is sometimes totally different from the initial message.

In this same sense, teenagers need to construct a sense of what their stories are, and this will be done by the things they see, the stories they hear, and the experiences they go through. Once all of these are placed together, a personal myth is created to help establish their personality. This will establish their narrative and the way they see the world—through the myths that they have constructed. Therefore, when they listen to myths that teachers tell them, they are able to relate because we are talking about real-life situations and implications in the hero's life.

Let me give you another example. You probably remember something from your childhood. However, have you ever been in a situation where you were with your family telling how you remembered the events, and they corrected you and told you things were not exactly as you imagined? This is not because you were trying to embellish something, but it was the way that you perceived and understood the situation. This led you to create a specific personal myth about it—it is a story that is not necessarily false, but it is made from your perspective.

Sometimes, when teenagers think about events that have gone on in their lives, they will create a specific narrative that fits into their perception at the time. Waddington says that "mythologizing your actions and giving them a heroic quality can be seen in the work of the religion scholar Mircea Eliade. He observed that for people to have meaningful lives, they must put their lives into a narrative, a story, a myth" (2009). Therefore, when we consider the importance of myths, we can say that they are essential for us to understand ourselves and how we fit into the world.

In a study carried out by Vlaicu & Voicu, 2013, they observed when applying narrative techniques and adapting the literature for teenagers, 79 percent of the students increased their cooperation in class, and 67 percent of teachers saw an increase in participation in the class. Furthermore, 40 percent of students were able to externalize and personify a problem, and 50 percent were able to develop a narrative about a problem they were going through. All by using myths and adapting the content of the classes. What is even more significant is that 60 percent of the students developed an interest in stories about themselves, and 70 percent found a different way to act in certain situations.

McGee (2018) adds to the discussion by stating that the most powerful kind of myths that can be created are the ones that come from our minds. It is there that we make sense of what has been taught in the mythological stories we have studied, and of the role of the others before us. Based on his analysis, we add our own adventures, thoughts, and ideas to the process, helping to unveil the secrets of the universe as we apply our knowledge. We can apply the context of personal myth to making sense of our actions due to trauma, for example, and this will help guide our daily actions. In a way, the "aha" moment that the hero will have in a myth will be a catalyst moment for the teenager to trigger transformation based on what they have experienced.

And it is at this moment that the awe comes. It is then that everything starts to make sense. This is because the teenager will see that their life story is not the representation of who they are, but a result of how they saw and interpreted the actions they have experienced in their lives. It is by the creation of personal myths that they grow and understand the world. This understanding, shaped by the actions students choose to take in their lives, greatly influences their future development as adults.

EMPOWERED EDUCATION: MY PERSONAL MYTHIC WAY

As a high school teacher, I've faced many challenging students. Some have been defiant, disinterested, or simply unengaged. But I've learned that students are within reach, no matter how unruly they seem. One approach that has worked wonders for me is incorporating ancient myths and legends into my lessons. I've always been fascinated by these stories, and I've found they can be a powerful tool for helping students understand complex ideas and themes.

One year, I had a challenging student named Juan. He disrupted class, talked back, and made my job difficult. Instead of punishing him, I decided to try a different approach.

At first, Juan was skeptical and made sarcastic comments whenever I mentioned the ancient Greeks. But as we delved deeper into the myths, I noticed a change in him. I began using ancient Greek myths and Afro-caribbean legends to illustrate essential concepts and themes, and I encouraged class discussions on what the stories meant in the context of the world around us.

Juan became interested in the stories and started asking questions and participating in discussions. He even submitted one of the class's most creative and thoughtful stories as an assignment. His story was about a hero who must face his inner demons to save his people, and it was full of symbolism and depth. When Juan presented his report to the class, I could see the pride and confidence in his eyes.

From that day forward, Juan was a changed student. Although he still had moments of noncompliance, I could tell he was more engaged and invested in the class. He was captivated by the power of myth and even approached me after class to ask questions about the stories we were studying.

This experience reminded me of the power of storytelling and myth-making in education. Even the most challenging students can be engaged and transformed with the right approach.

5

MARVEL!

> "He who can no longer pause to wonder and stand rapt in awe is as good as dead; his eyes are closed."
>
> — ALBERT EINSTEIN

Do you need help managing your classroom and engaging your students? Do you feel you need to be more motivated and inspired? If so, it's time to tap into the power of awe-inspiring educational moments.

Research has shown that experiences that evoke awe moments can have a profound impact on our lives. They can increase engagement, curiosity, open-mindedness, and improve our ability to retain information and solve problems. Creating opportunities for awe-inspiring experiences in your classroom can transform your teaching and greatly benefit your students.

In this chapter, we'll explore the importance of awe moments and how they can be incorporated into classroom management strategies. You'll discover personal stories and anecdotes that illustrate the incredible power of awe moments in a classroom setting. I'll show you how to align this concept with your teaching practice and classroom management to create a positive and engaging learning environment.

So if you're ready to unlock the full potential of your classroom and transform your students' lives, read on. You'll learn how awe-inspiring experiences can help you achieve your teaching goals and create a classroom that inspires and motivates you and your students.

AWE AS A FACTOR OF WELL-BEING

As a person directly connected to the world of arts, I can say that I have experienced several sublime moments in my life when I was filled with awe. As I traveled, studied, and performed, I have been lucky enough to feel a sense of awe at several moments. And let me tell you something: These moments make a difference in our lives and allow us to create memories forever. However, awe is more than making memories. When we experience something that truly defies our wildest expectations, it has the power to redirect our lives. As Richard Sima (2022) would put it, awe "produces little earthquakes in the mind."

According to Sima, the experience of awe makes our problems feel small by comparison, which enables us to lead happier and more fulfilling lives. This does not mean that you have to go to the moon or launch a rocket. The sense of awe can be experienced by merely observing our everyday lives in new ways. Awe is everywhere; to experience it, we must learn how to be open to the full range of lessons that life has to offer us.

"Feeling small makes us feel humbled (thereby lessening selfish tendencies like entitlement, arrogance, and narcissism). And feeling small and humbled makes us want to engage with others and feel more connected to others" (DiGiulio, 2019). When this happens, our mood improves, our social connections are enhanced, and we feel more generous and cooperative. In all the research I have read about feeling awe, there was not one negative thought associated with the feeling.

If you have ever been to the Grand Canyon, for example, you might have experienced this feeling. Or maybe you experienced it when looking at artwork in a museum. Maybe you have felt goosebumps by listening to an orchestra play. No matter what it was that made the hairs on the back of your neck stand up, you will probably never forget it. And every time you remember what the experience was like, you will have a feeling of well-being.

These astounding moments have a rejuvenating effect on the mind. Patients who show signs of PTSD, for example, are known to benefit from awe-inspiring moments. Furthermore, they have a genuine impact on our physical health and the way our body responds to certain situations. "Awe has health benefits that include releasing the feel-good hormone oxytocin, slowing our heart rate, and deepening our breathing" (Hillary, 2023). The benefits go on and on as research develops and scientists become closer to this feeling that we can say is indescribable.

Most importantly, when we feel awe, we go through a shift in the way that we perceive ourselves. We gain perspective, meaning, and purpose. Regardless of the form in which you have chosen to pursue this feeling, it will be important in determining your actions and the way that you see situations. Therefore, it is essential to always keep searching for the extraordinary. This is the best way to develop a sense of purpose, especially when it concerns our attitudes and the way we relate to students in the classroom.

To truly understand the role of awe in the classroom, we should first examine how it influences other areas of our society such as art, science and architecture. These will reveal an important link, as you will soon see, to the role of myth in the student development of purpose, and how this can be positive for their personal growth.

TRANSCENDING LIMITS: THE POWER OF AWE MOMENTS

In the book *Pathways to Bliss*, Joseph Campbell explains that one of the primary functions of myth is to provoke a sense of awe, mystery, and gratitude for the ultimate secret of being. This feeling of surprise or wonder, also known as the "aha effect," is considered the optimal objective of mystics, artists, and scientists. It's an experience in which the recipient of an artistic or scientific work spontaneously marvels. For a moment, their mind enters a state where all dogmatic knowledge is suspended. The observer perceives something beyond their usual knowledge but cannot explain it in words.

This overwhelming experience or awe moment is not limited to artistic or scientific works, but also occurs in those who listen to sacred music or any musical genre that evokes a sensation in the receiver. Campbell also notes that the quality or virtue of marveling at what is narrated in a mythological story is sufficient to awaken fervor in people and unite them in the same feeling.

The awe moment is the spontaneous, overwhelming feeling that a person feels when experiencing something beautiful, novel, or profound, like an artistic work. It could also be described as a flash of the transcendental. The awe moment may also be recognizable to some religious traditions as "a remembrance of God." This remembrance is considered the quintessence of every virtue and constitutes the whole point of the human state. It's comparable to the unconscious state in human beings, who instinctively seek to attune themselves to the Divine, to a truth or reality that is larger than themselves. This reality cannot be understood through reasoning alone, but can be perceived and intuitively understood by the individual.

The shock or surprise that students could experience when reading or listening to mirific incidents narrated by their teacher directly relates to one of the fundamental functions of mythological narratives. According to Campbell, myths primarily awaken people's consciousness. This "awakening" implies subtly recognizing a transcendent truth or reality that exists beyond intellectual understanding. The awakening of consciousness that Campbell alludes to could sometimes have its origin in the awe moment or the surprise that the recipients of mythological stories may have experienced.

From the vantage point of the Perennialist School of Thought, awe constitutes a mystical experience. Humans generally desire to have mystical experiences, even if most people are unaware of them. From this perspective, if presented effectively, the fantastic events narrated in your classroom or implemented in your instruction could produce a sense of wonder in some students.

Overall, the awe moment and the transcendent truth or reality it may reveal can be powerful tools for educators seeking to engage and inspire their students. However, creating awe moments isn't just about inspiring our students. It is also about reigniting our passion for teaching. When we approach our lessons with wonder and curiosity, we can tap into our creativity and find new ways to engage our students. We can break free from the limitations of our thinking and discover new possibilities for ourselves and our students.

So if you're feeling stuck in your teaching career or struggling with classroom management, remember that the power of the awe moment is within your reach. By embracing the wonder and mystery of the world around you, you can inspire your students, reignite your passion for teaching, and discover new possibilities for yourself and your students.

IGNITING WONDER: THE POWER OF AWE MOMENTS IN THE CLASSROOM

In the previous chapter, we explored the purposes of myths and their potential benefits when used in the classroom. You may wonder how myths and the awe they inspire can positively impact learning and teaching. Irving (2019) states, "Myth and ritual provide ample fodder for our sense of awe."

Recall the explanation of Campbell's theory on the importance of myths and how they lead students to that aha! moment. These awe moments, full of wonder, open their minds to new perspectives and help them appreciate the beauty and significance of their learning journey. These awe moments occur when students encounter a revelation or feeling they can't quite explain, yet whose importance they can appreciate. Such experiences can give them a new sense of meaning, making it a pivotal moment. As a teacher, you can spark these transformative moments and change their lives forever.

To better understand the importance of awe, let's revisit the initial question: Why do children go to school? As educators, we may emphasize the necessity of learning subjects like math, science, and history for their future. However, this might not convey the more profound meaning some students need. Consider the disruptive but brilliant student who excels academically yet struggles behaviorally. Do they not see the purpose in school because they lack awe-inspiring moments that make learning more meaningful?

It's time to empower your students by inviting awe into your classroom. The absence of wonder can lead to feelings of meaninglessness, which, as Zakrzewski (2013) points out, contributes to rising depression and suicide rates among youth. By contrast, students who find purpose and meaning in their education reap immediate rewards and understand the lifelong benefits. Embrace the magic of awe and myths, and transform your classroom into a place where learning becomes a life-changing adventure. Let the wonders of the universe, the depths of history, and the marvels of science inspire you and your students, guiding them toward endless possibilities and success.

The key takeaway is that students who find a purpose in their lives often experience a sense of awe, realizing something larger than themselves is at play. This realization prompts them to seek a greater purpose and understand the bigger picture in life. Myths can serve as an essential tool for helping students discover their purpose and create these awe-inspiring moments that transform their lives.

However, as Zakrzewski (2013) points out, teachers must recognize that not all students may be ready or willing to experience awe. Some individuals may be resistant to changing their perspective on the world.

> Accepting that your efforts to inspire awe in students may only resonate with some is essential. Keltner discovered that not all individuals are prone to awe—particularly those who prefer to maintain their current worldview. Nevertheless, this should not deter teachers

from attempting to create awe-inspiring student experiences (para. 18).

As an educator, you should embrace your inner strength and remain steadfast in your quest to inspire, awe, and motivate your students while sharing the gift of knowledge. You are a guiding light in their lives, with the power to shape their futures. Recall those moments when you experienced your own epiphanies—among them a profound sense of awe that revealed your true purpose: to teach, guide, and prepare others for the world. This realization is a beacon of inspiration that can guide you through even the most challenging days. Remember, you have within you the ability to kindle awe and wonder in the hearts of your students, nurturing their potential and leading them toward a future filled with endless possibilities. Hold on to this truth, and continue to strive for excellence as an educator, reigniting your passion and purpose each day.

Again, dear educator, let's think about the boundless sense of awe that young children effortlessly experience when faced with the unknown, such as a simple magic trick. They see a dancer and, captivated by the beauty of their movement, strive to replicate the performance. Their innocent curiosity drives them to embrace a purpose—learning, understanding, and growing. Young children marvel with astonishment when confronted with something they cannot explain. This demonstrates that our ability to experience awe is innate. As we age, we often lose this sense of wonder as we become more skeptical of the world.

As guiding lights in students' lives, it is crucial to rekindle the flames of awe and wonder that once burned brightly. The public school system's obsolete structure and sometimes rigid approach can inadvertently smother these embers. At times, instead of motivating students and helping them find purpose, the educational system may unintentionally diminish their motivation by failing to provide the extraordinary experiences they enjoyed when they were younger learners.

It's important to note that not all students will be awestruck by the same things; their interests will vary. As a teacher, it's your responsibility to discover what inspires awe in each individual. Recognize that each student's heart responds to different rhythms of inspiration; your sacred task is to find what awakens their souls. Also, be aware the awe experiences are spontaneous, not mechanical. Our job is to provide them with sufficient elements.

To spark wonder and awe in classroom activities and to address or minimize classroom management issues, we must consider the structure of the public school system we work for. The obsolete public school system in New York City, which is the only system I know well, does not adequately promote the experience of wonder as an educational tool, except perhaps in the early years—kindergarten, first, and second grade. As students progress in their education, the system tends to become more rigid, less flexible, and increasingly boring, contributing to the lack of motivation in many students.

Our goal should be to teach students using tools to encourage them to develop a sense of purpose and find meaning in their lives. Some students may have difficulty experiencing awe, often due to external circumstances affecting their school life or their challenging environments. However, as Bidshahri (2017) notes, effective education is less about delivering content knowledge and more about equipping students with the skills and values required for active learning, enabling them to find knowledge and inspiration independently. It is not merely about what you teach, but how you do it.

AWE-INSPIRED CHANGE

It is crucial that we, as educators, bring back the 'awe factor' to the classroom and recognize the need to transform the learning environment. Doing so ensures that our students are engaged and find purpose in their education. Our classrooms need to rekindle that sense of awe, becoming spaces where students remain engaged and discover meaning in their learning. As the drivers of change, we must take the initiative to make a difference in their lives and the current educational system. As catalysts for change, we can shape our student's lives and the educational system itself.

When children and teenagers experience awe-inspiring moments within the classroom, their lives and perspectives undergo a transformative shift. They begin to unlock their true potential and develop a newfound eagerness to embrace life's vast possibilities. Koehler (2023) eloquently stated, "As children encounter awe-inspiring moments, they learn to approach challenges with an open mind and a willingness to explore life's vast possibilities." Embrace the power of awe moments, and let it be the driving force that empowers your students to thrive both inside and outside the classroom.

A paradigm shift in how students perceive school is long overdue, and as educators, we must be the ones to initiate it. Move beyond monotonous lessons focused solely on content delivery and learn to captivate students with your knowledge and life experiences. Demonstrate the awe-inspiring wonders of the world that can reshape their perspectives and help them connect with the extraordinary within themselves. Providing students with more meaningful learning experiences will benefit you as their teacher, create changes in their classroom behavior, and inspire profound transformations within the students themselves.

To ignite this transformation, help students grasp the incredible possibilities. Acknowledge their individual learning needs and channel their insatiable curiosity to see the value of being in school. Encourage students to derive pleasure from learning by feeling joy and empowerment through the content they access and the information they acquire. As Sheninger (2016) suggests, "awe can be cultivated in personal and personalized learning opportunities where the main motivation comes from student agency."

However, fostering awe in the classroom may sometimes take work. Recall the discussion about teachers serving as sources of motivation and role models and the significance of myths in helping students discover their authentic selves and purpose. Some students may need help to identify what truly inspires them; this is where your role as a teacher becomes vital.

This is the juncture where teachers can make a significant impact. Bidshahri (2017) states, "Effective education is less about delivering content knowledge to young minds and more about equipping them with the skills and values required to find that knowledge and inspiration on their own, through active learning." Adapt your teaching methods to engage students in learning and foster a genuine interest in the material. This shift in approach can potentially transform disruptive behavior in the classroom.

Pandora's Box and the Periodic Table

Consider an example that you might easily relate to. Imagine you are a chemistry teacher. Teaching students about formulas, catalysts, and reactions may only sometimes engage them; they might even be bored. However, you could modify your lesson plan and introduce the topic through a mythological tale. In that case, you can undoubtedly capture their attention, especially if you creatively present the myth, fairy tale, or story. A fitting story from ancient Greek mythology to introduce a periodic table lesson in a chemistry class would be the tale of Pandora's Box.

According to Greek mythology, Pandora was the first woman created by the gods. Zeus, the king of the gods, gifted her a box (or a jar, in some versions) with instructions not to open it. Driven by curiosity, Pandora opened the box, releasing all the world's troubles, diseases, and miseries, leaving only Hope behind.

This myth can serve as an analogy for the periodic table. Just as Pandora's Box contained different elements that affected the world in various ways, the periodic table organizes chemical elements, each with its unique properties and characteristics. Some elements benefit human life and progress, while others can be dangerous or cause harm.

By introducing the periodic table through this myth, you can pique your students' curiosity, encourage them to explore the vast range of elements, and understand the potential consequences of how they interact. It also serves as a reminder of the importance of learning about these elements to use them responsibly and for the betterment of our lives.

Once you have captured their attention and interest, you can demonstrate how a chemical reaction works, which may instill a sense of awe in some students. The primary reason is that they will not only be listening to an ancient story and the new content presented in class, but they will also be able to experiment and witness the science happening right before their eyes.

Incorporating awe-inspiring moments in your lessons can transform students' engagement and help them find purpose in the classroom. By stimulating their interest through hands-on experiences and practical applications, you create opportunities for students to connect deeply with the subjects. Think about your teaching strategies and how you can foster wonder and curiosity.

For example, instead of merely teaching plant structures in biology, consider going out with your students in the fields or parks around the school building and collecting leaves for in-class examinations. Such simple changes in approach can elevate student engagement and passion for learning and allow you to interact with them in environments other than the classroom. Your creativity should drive these innovations, leading you to ask: How can I engage my students? How can I help them find purpose? How can I impact their lives? Answering these questions might be challenging, but embracing the challenge will bring positive results.

Reflect on your initial motivations for becoming a teacher, tapping into memories of awe-inspiring moments in your learning journey. Sharing those experiences with your students can transcend the boundaries of traditional education, fostering an environment where detailed observations and deep exploration become the norm.

Be open to expanding your teaching methods and embracing new perspectives. This may require tapping into other abilities, knowledge, or discussions, and may demand energy and effort. However, the outcome will be worth it as you witness the amazement in your students' eyes and the changes in their approach to learning.

As a driver of change, consider adding awe to your classroom and empowering your students to experience the remarkable benefits of wonder and curiosity. Embrace the challenge, inspire your students, and allow yourself to be awed by their growth and transformation.

This might mean that you have to tap into other abilities, knowledge, or discussions. It could mean that you will have to change your perception of the classroom. Perhaps it will demand from you an energy that you feel you no longer have. Nevertheless, it is worth a try. The effort will bring you positive results. There is nothing more satisfying for a teacher than to see the amazement in their students' eyes because of what they are teaching. Allow **yourself** to be touched by the fabulous sense of awe that you will feel once you see the difference that you can make as a driver of change. Awe your students, but also allow yourself to be awed in the process.

AWING STUDENTS

One of my students was particularly disruptive during a unit lesson on the Spanish subjunctive mood, a notoriously complex topic. I was well aware of this student's troublesome history. I wanted to find a way to encourage this student to engage while also delivering the challenging Spanish grammar topic. My solution was to find a way to connect with him during the lesson. To do so, I memorized his date of birth. The next time he disrupted class, I paused the lesson and turned to him with a theatrical air, to say, "I see why you're acting up... I sense you are an Aries."

He was stunned and inquired how I knew that. With a knowing smile, I replied, "Your energy, I can sense it." The lesson took an unexpected turn as I spent the next few minutes discussing astrology, its relationship with astronomy, and how these were once considered an exact science during the Middle Ages.

After this engaging digression, my once-disruptive student became more focused and attentive. He never found out how I "knew so much about him" and very often told his classmates and other students in the school (that sometimes came to see me during my lunch period to talk about life and ask me questions) that I could read people's thoughts. My approach demonstrated that I cared for him and showcased an impressive intellect, fostering newfound respect. The interaction exemplified the importance of educators finding inventive ways to connect with their students, even in challenging situations, to improve the classroom atmosphere and facilitate learning. Of course, I don't have such power, just the power of Marvel education.

High school students often have a curiosity about their teachers' lives. This natural curiosity could be used to establish connections and get to know students better. One day, a typically disruptive and angry student asked me, "Where are you from?"

I replied, "I don't know where I was born."

The student, intrigued, questioned, "Why?"

I continued with a captivating tale. "Once upon a time, a woman in Latin America gave birth to a beautiful baby. One day, while they were at the park, someone snatched her baby and replaced it with an ugly one. That ugly baby was me. The kindhearted woman raised me, never finding her real child, and I never found my true family. So, I don't really know where I was born."

After some time, I completely forgot that I had shared the story with my students. Although I had forgotten, my students had not! One of them brought it up again when she attended a parent/teacher conference with her mother. Even before introducing ourselves, I heard her say to her mother, "Mom, look! That was the teacher I told you was exchanged for another when he was a baby."

As a high school teacher, I had a particularly challenging Spanish 5 class, filled with difficult students, some of whom were involved in gangs. The leader of a prominent Bronx gang was in my class, and his influence was apparent. He would not come to class often; once in a while he would come to the classroom and would sit in the back of the room, by himself.

One day after class, after everyone left the room, the gang leader approached me with a bundle of cash containing $20, $50 and $100 bills. He wanted me to take the money in exchange for helping him pass the class. Instead of accepting the bribe, in a matter of seconds I thought right on the spot, and without thinking much, I offered him an alternative solution. I told him: "You don't need to give me money to pass this class. All you have to do is come to class every day, help me keep the class quiet, and I will ensure you pass at the end of the marking period."

To my surprise, he agreed. He committed to attending class regularly and assisting me in maintaining order. His presence alone was enough to keep the other gang-affiliated students in check. Whenever any student misbehaved, all it took was a glance from him, and they would immediately stop.

From that day on, my once-challenging class transformed into the best I had ever taught. The student who led the gang assisted me in managing his classmates and at the same time set a shining example through his unwavering commitment to completing homework every day. This experience demonstrated how effective communication and understanding can yield positive outcomes, even in tricky or peculiar situations. In this instance, I managed to turn a potentially challenging situation into a marvel of collaboration and classroom management, revolutionizing not only the dynamics of the class but also the learning experience for all students involved.

As we gracefully transition into Chapter 6, we will delve into the power of the Socratic Dialogue, a teaching method that fosters deep thinking and meaningful discussions. This technique will further empower you, dear teacher, to unleash the extraordinary potential within your students, paving the way for stimulating and engaging classroom conversations.

6

SOCRATIC DIALOGUE: UNLEASHING MARVELOUS CLASSROOM CONVERSATIONS

 "Education is the kindling of a flame, not the filling of a vessel."

— SOCRATES

You have likely applied it even if you have never heard about the Socratic Dialogue. Moreover, your students have probably used this methodology and need to realize it. Socratic Dialogue is a conversation between two or more individuals where one person asks questions to stimulate critical thinking and encourage the other person to articulate their ideas. It is named after the ancient Greek philosopher Socrates, who used it to engage his disciples in discussions about ethics, politics, and other philosophical topics.

In modern education, Socratic Dialogue promotes critical thinking and problem-solving skills. While listening attentively, teachers ask questions to motivate students to think critically and examine their beliefs and assumptions. Students can respond to inquiries and consider alternative perspectives by reflecting on and understanding a subject. Socratic Dialogue is an effective way to determine the accuracy of reasoning and to understand someone's thought process, while helping them be aware of their own process. It creates a safe and respectful environment for dialogue and encourages students to explore complex ideas. This chapter will discuss strategies for developing practical questions and creating a productive dialogue environment.

To facilitate discussion about literature, teachers can use Socratic Dialogue. For example, when teaching Homer's Odyssey, an English teacher might start by asking open-ended questions about the epic poem's themes, such as "What are some of the major themes in The Odyssey?" and follow up with more specific questions like "How does Odysseus demonstrate his cunning in the face of danger?" or "What do we learn about ancient Greek culture and values through The Odyssey?".

As the conversation continues, teachers should listen carefully and ask more questions that encourage critical thinking. For instance, "How can Odysseus' resilience serve us, nowadays, as an example to stoically handle social and emotional challenges?" This approach will help students develop their critical thinking skills and engage with complex ideas productively.

Throughout the dialogue, teachers should listen attentively and use their ideas to guide the conversation in new directions. By using Socratic Dialogue in this way, teachers can create a safe and respectful environment for dialogue that encourages students to explore complex ideas.

However, the Socratic method should not be seen as a form of debate, since the primary objective here is that the individual or group finds a satisfactory answer to the questions that are being asked. It is a similar process of breaking down something into smaller parts, and, in this case, the questions start from a larger perspective and are narrowed down until reaching a specific detail. When you think about this process, it is a skill teachers can practice to engage their students in conversation.

Therefore, we could say of the Socratic method "The basic form is a series of questions formulated as tests that are intended to help a person or group discover their beliefs about a given topic, exploring definitions and seeking to characterize general characteristics shared by various particular instances" (Hehe, 2021).

However, before we look deeper into how the Socratic method can be used in teaching, let's take a look at some of the concepts that must be applied to it in order to ensure its success. The Socratic Dialogue is composed of different "classes" of questions that can range from those that ask for more clarification to those that will explore the point of view of the person who is answering (Schadt, 2021). These include questions related to:

- Identifying the reasons why the other person has a certain thought
- Assessing if the other understands the implications and consequences of a thought

- Clarifying concepts
- Questioning their perspectives and point of view on a certain subject
- Understanding if there are any underlying assumptions in the rationale
- Questioning the importance and relevance of the question that has been asked

During this process, the teacher, or the individual who is asking the questions, should not disagree with the person but rather try to make them rationalize what they are saying by **asking more questions**, so they can identify the line of thought. This means that they will explore the individual's point of view and be able to assess the thought process. However, for this to be effective, the process must be well structured, where random questions are avoided and the questioning party does not try to answer the questions for the other.

In addition to this, they themselves should develop rationale. This means avoiding passing judgment or giving them alternate lines of thought that could lead them to deviate from the initial line of thought. Now, this might seem very familiar, especially if you have seen a therapist in person or on a television show. If this was your first thought when you read my description, you are certainly on the right path. This is because the Socratic method is specially designed to help understand others, which is the main objective of a therapy session. However, it is not only limited to this area. Law enforcement uses it, lawyers use it in trials, teachers use it in the classroom, Zen masters and life coaches as well; and what do you know, even parents use it with their children when they want to get to the bottom of a certain issue.

Furthermore, if you have related this method to the act of "playing dumb," then you also have that right. This form of logic is exactly that. You "play dumb" to ask questions and inquire about things that you want to understand, and make the person get to the bottom of their beliefs. However, in the same way that you have probably had a student "play dumb" in the classroom and ask you questions and more questions about a subject as a way to defy you, you must also know that applying the same concept in teaching can be extremely beneficial, as we will now see.

TRANSFORMATIVE PEDAGOGY OF THE SOCRATIC METHOD

Delic and Bećirović (2016) assert that the Socratic method is a practical pedagogical approach as it aligns with Socrates' goal of empowering individuals to become masters of their thoughts and state of being. This approach has been instrumental in shaping the minds of notable students, including the renowned philosopher Plato.

Contrasting to what is stated by Resilient Educator (2012), "This method works well in subjective disciplines like philosophy, art, the humanities, or even the ethics of science, but it may not be the best teaching method for objective disciplines like mathematics or science," my belief is that this method can be applied to all the educational disciplines. Even if there are clear boundaries between subjects, we can, by using real-life examples and experiences, even myths, if you will, help students see the purpose or identify meaning through this technique.

Despite being a well-known method of teaching, the Socratic method has undergone some changes since it was initially applied, especially so that it can be adopted by teachers from the most varied subjects. This means that the concept of the Socratic method can be divided into the "classic" and the "modern" method. However, this does not mean that one is outdated and the other is better. It simply means that there are different ways to adapt and apply them in the classroom.

When you consider the classic method, know that it is related to obtaining short answers that are related to a specific intended point. This means that conversations or the introduction of new subjects could be cut short—it is intended only to define the topics that will be discussed and establish a guideline, rather than obtaining the sense of a deeper meaning. Delic and Bećirovic (2016) argue that the classical method

> Prepares people to think and to improve themselves through increased understanding. This phase deconstructs people's previous understanding, leaves them being less sure of what they previously knew, or helps them be conscious of their ignorance of a certain topic at all, helping them know what they do not know (para. 3, Classic Socratic Method section).

The other method, known as the modern method, is more about progressing question by question until the final answer is reached, as we have seen in the example I gave you before. This method enables the person who is asking questions to delve deeper into the matter in question and helps the person who is answering to develop critical thinking. Therefore, when we talk about applying the Socratic method in school and throughout the learning process, we are really talking about applying this one.

I want you to think once again about a classroom situation. How many times have you involved your students in the lesson you were giving? How many times have you asked them questions to participate in the class rather than just telling them the information? How many times have you instigated them into asking questions about what you were teaching?

As I mentioned earlier, I do believe that this method can be applied in all the disciplines that are taught in school—it is just a matter of adapting the content. Once again, I understand how the process can seem to work better in those disciplines that are more objective, such as math. However, when you apply them to other topics that are more subjective, you might have the benefit of aiding your students in the process of thought. For example, there may not be a specific answer, but rather something that they must reflect upon.

Therefore, I could say that the key to successfully implementing the Socratic method in teaching is to **know what you are asking**. This means that you must prepare for both what you are going to ask and what the students will potentially answer. Keep in mind that the second is not as important as the first—it will be your ability to conduct the questioning that will determine the way the discussion will go with your class.

At the same time, you must beware of the negative aspects of applying this strategy. As claimed by Delic and Bećirovic (2016), "Those who are against the Socratic method claim that the teachers who use it wait for students to make mistakes to criticize their imperfect answers, exposing them to public degradation, humiliation, and ridicule." But this does not necessarily need to be the rule, but rather the exception. When you study before applying the questions and have a clear teaching path established, it will definitely bring more benefits than damage to the classroom.

The main idea here is to provoke the thought process, and not discourage the student from thinking they are being something of a "smarty-pants." The idea, after all, **is** to get the students to develop a thought process and analyze their own line of logic. Thus, by applying the Socratic method in the classroom, you will be teaching **more** than the theme of the lesson, but a way for students to establish their rationale as well.

And when this happens, as they reach this aha moment, can you guess what will happen? You probably can. If you guessed that they will undergo a moment of awe, then you are correct. The realization of a correct line of thought and enabling them to reach these conclusions just by asking questions will give them the opportunity to feel like the hero in the myth—they reach a point where they have a "lightbulb" moment in which they have an idea and are able to act to find a solution. And this, dear reader, is a game-changing feeling.

HARNESSING THE SOCRATIC METHOD FOR EFFECTIVE TEACHING

If the wheels are already turning inside your head and you are thinking about ways you can implement the Socratic method in your classroom, let me be the first to say: Way to go! I like the way you are thinking. In this section, I want to talk some more about how this method can be applied and how it may not just be something to help with your lessons, but also with disruptive students.

The first thing you should consider when thinking about asking these questions is that they have to be open-ended, meaning they must be the path to asking more questions based on the answers. This means that the teacher will continuously ask questions to the students until a deeper understanding is reached about the subject. The essential part is to always let the students do most of the talking, limiting you, the teacher, to asking questions and clarifying any points on which they may have doubts (Llego, 2022).

If you intend to start this process, the first thing you should do is explain to the students what your teaching method is and what is expected of them. And be prepared: In the beginning, the students might not understand what you are doing. Miller (2021), tells the story about how she brought this to the classroom and how it made her students feel the first time the method was applied.

The first day that I questioned random students back-to-back-to-back, they were terrified. Just like in law school, I allowed them to have their reading and their notes for reference, and I asked them questions and probed for a rationale. They were spooked. Some kids were visibly anxious, and the stress for some became too much. We paused. I told my students to take a breath.

I explained to them that this method is stressful, and I also warned them that some use this instructional technique in ways that are disrespectful, harmful, and unjust. However, I assured them that our classroom was a training ground for the rigorous style of instruction and demanding nature of textual exegesis they'd experience beyond high school.

I also told them that I believed they were more than capable of showing what they knew. With that, my students grew calmer and we continued. The next week we did it, more students were prepared. They had their notes, their books were highlighted, and they expected that they'd get called on (para. 9-11).

Although there are many approaches to the matter in question, I usually follow the format that is also proposed by Llego (2022), who recommends the following steps:

1. Ask a question to start off the discussion, and make this question open-ended.

2. Motivate the students to participate, reflect, and also ask them questions to clarify any doubts they might have and to help them rationalize.
3. Reinforce the assumptions they make and ask questions based on them so they can be clear as to what they are answering.
4. The next step is very important to the process, which is that you must not give them any answers. You must allow them to think for themselves and reach a conclusion based on their own rationale.
5. Conclude the sessions by making a general summary of what was explored and reinforce the main points of discussion, which will enable them to easily remember the information.

Throughout the process, you should always keep in mind the different approaches that you should adopt, depending on whether you are dealing with a group or with one individual. For example, if you are dealing with the class, you might want to do as Miller did in the example and allow the students to keep their notes open for consultation. It may also be interesting to call out the students based on your discretion, making those who seem less willing to participate involved in the questioning.

Still, when speaking to a group, I usually find it favorable to walk around the class as I am probing the questions. This makes the students pay attention to the movement, and it also gives them the feeling that you could call on them at any time (Miller, 2021). When you do this, you are giving the classroom what several authors mention as a "productive discomfort." This means that you will respectfully correct them if they say something wrong and continue to question them if you see they are able to continue.

Now, if you are dealing with a student on a one-on-one basis, there are a few other approaches that you could use. And this is where I take the opportunity to mention that the Socratic method does not necessarily need to be applied **only** throughout the learning process. You can use it to solve problems among students, inquire about one's disciplinary issues, help them solve a problem, and much more. Depending on the situation, you can use a tone of concern, a serious voice, or any other that you think is necessary to apply to the situation.

In all cases, the key is to be patient when waiting for an answer to one of your questions. In addition to this, learn how to be okay with silence—sometimes the student you are asking might need some time to think. Think about a student who has been undisciplined in your class. You may want to speak to them in private after school to understand what is going on. Once again, you must remember that some of them might be coming from toxic environments. Some students are so focused on surviving their life circumstances that they don't have the time or energy to reflect on how they are affected. That's where you can help them.

In these situations, when you are dealing with personal matters, you must be careful not to "poke" them too much, so that they feel uncomfortable. You will need to read their body language and their response to your questions to understand if you should continue or not. Depending on the problem, you might want to tell them a story in which you or a known person went through a similar situation and how it was solved. The key here will be to help this student identify the reasons for the misbehavior. By doing this, you may understand the underlying causes and be able to help them **within** the classroom while you are carrying out your lesson.

Finally, you must remember that this method is **all about keeping your students engaged**. Think about how you will factor in that moment of awe in your student. The moment in which they realize that they **are** able to learn and understand the content by using critical thinking. If you are still unsure how this would work for you, try bringing to class a quote, a real-life story, or a **myth**. Don't be afraid to explore topics that might seem "crazy," but hold deeper meanings beneath the surface of the text.

Tap into your journey as a teacher and all the knowledge you have gained down the road of your life and help **them** understand, by asking questions, how this can be useful in their lives. Use it as a respectful tool to show them the fabulous power of reasoning, to ask questions to solve problems, and to think about alternatives. By doing this, not only will you be creating a connection with them, but you might also learn something new in the process, who knows?

THE EXTRAORDINARY POWER OF DIALOGUE

I have come to understand that there are times when dealing with difficult situations calls for more than just imposing authority. One day, a case that called for a more nuanced approach was presented, and I had to rely on the Socratic dialogue method to navigate it.

At a school in Queens, two of my students, Marcus and Willy, had a terrible argument in the cafeteria, which had escalated into a violent altercation. By the time they reached my classroom, Willy had smacked Marcus in the face and fled inside. When I saw Marcus's anger, I knew I had to act quickly to prevent the situation from escalating further.

When Willy entered the classroom, I locked the door behind him and stepped outside to talk to Marcus. He was fuming with rage and was determined to get revenge. The situation was getting out of hand, and even the intervention of a school administrator and security officer didn't make a difference. But I knew there had to be a way to help Marcus see reason. I employed the Socratic dialogue method, asking him open-ended questions and prompting him to reflect on the situation. Gradually, he began to calm down and opened up about the root of his anger.

With patience and empathy, I was able to help Marcus see that violence wasn't the answer. We discussed alternative ways of resolving the problem with Willy, and I convinced him to go to the Dean's office with one of the school administrators.

The Socratic dialogue approach helped me connect with Marcus on a deeper level and understand the reasons behind his behavior. By listening to him and engaging him in a constructive conversation, I was able to de-escalate the situation and help him find a non-violent way to resolve the conflict.

Ultimately, this experience taught me the power of the Socratic dialogue method and how it can help students in difficult situations. It reinforced my belief that empathy, patience, and open communication are essential in resolving conflicts and building positive relationships with students.

As we move on to the final chapter of this first book, I want you to reflect on all the tools and resources that I have given you so far. Are you able to identify a common element? If your answer is that the focus is **on the student**, then you are once again correct. As you will see in the next and last chapter, the common element between all the students in whatever school you are teaching in, is that they yearn for attention, for love, to be seen. This begs the question: *When was the last time that you looked, really looked, at your students?*

THE POWER OF LOVE IN THE CLASSROOM: EMPOWERING STUDENT VOICE AND IDENTITY

> "When you study great teachers... you will learn much more from their caring and hard work than from their style."
>
> — WILLIAM GLASSER

As a NYC public school teacher, I have worked with many students over the years. However, it is the disruptive students who have taught me the most. I have realized that most of them are simply seeking the attention they do not receive at home. This resonates with a quote by Nicholas A. Ferroni, who once said, "Students who are loved at home come to school to learn. Students who aren't... come to school to be loved" (Flippen Group, 2016).

It is heartbreaking to witness the impact of toxic home environments on students. Many students I have taught have experienced financial and food insecurity, parents in jail, divorce, drugs, gangs, and more. These students are often labeled as "problematic" by other teachers, administration, and caretakers. However, I have found that taking the time to converse and understand what is going on in their lives can make all the difference. By showing them that we care, we can help them feel valued and supported and create a positive learning environment that empowers their voices and identities.

As teachers, we understand that our job requires working even when all the information and resources we need aren't readily available to us. We face stress and burnout and often feel unsupported by administrators. However, we have a responsibility to start the process of change. By making our students the central characters of the story of the education system, we can build the kind of communities that empower them. We can make a difference in their lives by showing them love, care, and understanding.

Let us take the time to understand our students. Let us show them love and care. Let us empower their voices and identities. Doing so can create a positive and supportive learning environment that helps them thrive. We have the power to make a difference in the lives of our students, and it is up to us to start the change. It may not be easy, but it is worth it. Together, we can create a better future for our students and for ourselves as educators. So let us take the first step and start the journey toward empowering our students, and ourselves, with the power of love in the classroom.

SCHOOL AS A VENUE OF LOVE

Let me ask you a question: When was the last time that you remembered your love for teaching? When was the last time you reminded yourself of the ideals that inspired you to become an educator in the first place? If you are not in a good place right now, it has probably been some time. Now, think about it for a moment: If you are not feeling the love, you are likely not showing it. And if you are not showing it, why should the students reciprocate positive feelings toward you? What are you giving **them**?

And while you may be teaching them the skills they need for the future, you may be missing something critical: Love. As several education experts point out, teachers who love what they do and incorporate this feeling into their lessons can significantly impact students' lives and positively change the educational system. Unfortunately, love is often considered a taboo topic in the American public school system, and it is rarely discussed openly. But caring is an expression of love, and one of the primary reasons people become educators.

As teachers, we must show our students that we care for them. Being present, actively listening, and seeing them for who they are is the best way to do this. Students respond positively when they feel valued and appreciated, even if we are strict, and we must limit their behavior occasionally. However, expressing love is not a mechanical process. It requires us to be at peace and in harmony with ourselves before we can synchronize with the flame of love and illuminate others. Bringing love and care into our teaching practices can create a positive and supportive learning environment that helps students thrive. We must remember that love and beauty cannot be evaluated traditionally. Still, they are critical components of education that we must embrace to make a real impact on our student's lives. Let's show our students that we care for them, that they are essential, and that they have the potential to achieve great things.

As educators, we are responsible for creating a positive and supportive learning environment that helps students thrive. We can show love and care in many ways, such as carrying out tutoring sessions, bringing in topics of interest, and checking on our students occasionally. By incorporating love and care into our teaching practices, we demonstrate to our students that they are important, valued, and worthy of our time and attention. These qualities are essential components of our students' learning journey, and it is up to us to prioritize them in our teaching practices.

For some students, the school may be the only place where they feel they belong and where it matters that they are there. They want to be seen, heard, loved, valued, praised, and cared for. They might be acting out because they are thirsty for attention, and poor or disruptive behavior can be a manifestation of this. As education expert Phillips points out, students who keep asking for help or dubbing on other students might seek genuine, loving, and positive attention they do not receive at home (Phillips, 2022).

Teachers must recognize that some students may not communicate their needs directly or in a way we might prefer. As Nguyen emphasizes, some students may act up to be heard. In these moments, we must tap into our love for teaching and become the mentors who guide our students through their own "Hero's Journey." By doing so, we can help them feel seen, heard, and valued, and unlock their full potential as they become the best version of themselves.

THE SELF AS A HERO

According to Campbell's *The Hero with a Thousand Faces*, heroes embody the highest ideals of their respective traditions, which concern all of humanity. Despite their differences, there are fundamental similarities between heroes like Gilgamesh, Agamemnon, Antigone, Lord Rama, Esther, Oedipus, Wonder Woman, and Superman. Each character is the focal point of a complex social, religious, and cultural paradigm. Each one represents the possibility of each person realizing the ideals that are important to their culture (or humanity as a whole). All these heroic narrations follow a universal structure that Campbell called the hero's journey or "monomyth." This journey consists of three phases: The exit, the initiation, and the return.

In such a universal model, heroes leave what is familiar, face challenges, and return home with newfound power to benefit their community. It is important not to lose sight of the fact that the "movement" of the hero, as it appears in any of its various forms, does not always constitute a literal transfer from one place to another since the journey can be psychological, as we can see happening with the protagonist of the novel *Ulysses* by James Joyce.

The monomyth, or the universal model of heroic adventure, emphasizes the importance of effort in achieving one's desired goal. It also gives supporters of a particular group or tradition hope to continue pursuing their objectives or ideals. Homeric heroes in the *Iliad* and *Odyssey*, such as Achilles and Odysseus, seek honor and glory through their combative and dangerous feats. This glory is reserved for those who consistently fulfill their duty as heroes. In the Bhagavad-Gītā (11:33) and the Quran (Surah 2:214), the universal concept of effort to achieve the Optimal Goal is emphasized, and conscious commitment to one's duty is seen as a fundamental element across religions and cultures. The idea that effort is necessary for well-being on physical, metaphysical, or psychic planes is universal.

Every day, we all experience our own heroic journeys. The monomyth or hero's journey metaphor can be applied to almost any human experience, even something as seemingly ordinary as breathing. For many people, breathing can be challenging, and to them, the experience is like a heroic trek; walking a few yards might represent a three-mile journey to a paralytic; activities such as getting out of bed, getting dressed, going to the supermarket, and dealing with difficult traffic and credit card issues while just trying to pay for the few items you purchased are ordinary examples of what could constitute a hero's journey. Leaving the comfort of your home to face these challenges in pursuing a simple goal, such as buying groceries, could be considered a heroic journey in its own right. Similarly, teachers experience their personal journey every morning when they go to work.

The concept of the monomyth can be applied to teachers' experiences as they face challenges and tests throughout their workday. Consider the example of Ms. Teach, a math teacher at an urban high school in Seattle. Her daily routine can be viewed through the lens of the hero's journey, with its three distinct phases. The first phase, "the exit," corresponds to Ms. Teach waking up early and going to work. Once at school, she faces various challenges, such as creating special assignments for students with learning problems, managing unruly behavior, dealing with administrative pressure, and having an unpleasant phone conversation with an irrational and disrespectful parent.

For Ms. Teach, all these challenges represent the second phase, "the initiation." In this phase, Ms. Teach must demonstrate patience, resilience, and courage to overcome each trial. Each challenge allows her to observe and reflect on her teaching practice, making necessary adjustments for improvement. The third and final phase, "the return," corresponds to Ms. Teach returning home as a changed person, having gained valuable experience and insights throughout the day. In this way, the hero's journey provides a valuable framework for understanding teachers' daily challenges and growth opportunities.

Every day, our students, like all individuals, embark on their own heroic journeys. Attending a school where they don't receive a quality education can be a challenge that jeopardizes their future opportunities. Negligent parents, bullying in their communities or schools, an unhealthy diet, and learning difficulties are just a few examples of the tests they might face. These experiences align with the phases of the monomyth outlined by Campbell.

We, mortal teachers, cannot perform miracles. We cannot always protect our students from suffering or adversity. However, understanding the situations that could distress the hearts of our students enables us to support them silently and provide them with tools to overcome their obstacles. Despite their challenges, we can help them continue pursuing their ideals, from test to test and victory to victory on their journey through life. By offering our support and guidance, we can empower them to grow, overcome adversity, and achieve their goals.

In the process of empowering our students to achieve greatness in their own lives, it is important that you, as an educator, be empowered and inspired. Ways a teacher can be inspired include seeking out professional development opportunities such as attending conferences, workshops, and training sessions. Additionally, staying up-to-date with the latest research and trends in education can help you improve your teaching practice. Seeking mentorship from experienced teachers or educational leaders can also provide valuable guidance and feedback.

You can also gather feedback from your students to improve your teaching. This can come from asking for their input on your teaching methods, activities, and assignments, as well as from your own observations. Self-reflection is a valuable tool for self-improvement.

Taking care of your physical and emotional well-being is also essential for being an effective teacher. Engage in self-care activities such as exercise, meditation, spending time in nature, or spending time with friends and family. By taking care of yourself, you can prevent burnout and better serve your students as a positive role model.

As teachers, it's important that we observe ourselves to ensure our teaching practices align with transcendent ideals. By being clear about our professional and personal objectives, we can see ourselves and our actions with total transparency. We must always strive for the common good of society and all of humanity. In this sense, educators are like heroes of the twenty-first century, inspiring students to work toward a better world. Like mythological heroes Arjuna, Aeneas, or Samson, we have the power to point out the possibility of a brighter future. Through self-reflection and alignment with transcendent ideals, we can continue to inspire and guide our students toward a better future.

BUILDING BRIDGES TO SUCCESS: THE MARVEL EDUCATION APPROACH

As you have seen, all of the steps up to now have led you to guide your students through the Hero's Journey. Through this process, they will experience the feeling of awe—of themselves and the teaching environment. Once you really start to "see" your students, understand them, and identify their unique needs, you can make a difference.

If your class is being disruptive and not listening, pay attention to them. If students lack motivation, look for sources of inspiration. If they cannot find meaning, teach them how to see what is relevant. Use myths to show them that change is possible and challenges can be overcome. Help them experience the extraordinary. Teach them how to question, how to think, and how to be the differential factor.

But, most of all, listen to your students—to what they are saying and are not saying. Speak **to** your class and not **at** them—show them that their presence in the classroom is important and their participation is essential. See these individuals for who they are—don't just look at them as a part of a job you are dissatisfied with because of all the problems you face. Finally, love your students and give them the attention they deserve. Show them that it is possible to be astonished with the school environment—that it is a wonderful place to be.

Overcome the tiredness, the lack of motivation, the temptation to give up on all the ideals you held dear when you first entered the teaching profession. Go back to that place where you felt a marvel with education and what it can do for our youth. Think what these individuals need to be successful and to become the productive adults that all of us need to create a healthy society. Remember the sublime feeling that you felt when you finally identified your calling, and that it was to help teach and make a difference in these kids' lives.

The key here is to remember that **the key to marvel education is meaningful learning**. Once you are able to see the marvelous things that you **can** do, that your students **are able** to achieve, and how this will **positively impact** society, you will find a new motivation. You will see your classroom change from misbehaved individuals to interested and engaged students. Participation will increase, motivation will be different, and better people will arise from this.

When you show your class how much you love to teach them, and when you demonstrate the positive impact that active learning can have in their lives, you will see them thrive in awe. You will see the marvelous change and remarkable improvements that result. When you teach a lesson taking students' needs into consideration, you change the environment, the atmosphere. You help them feel something that they might not have anywhere else.

Lastly, when you "give" to the students, they will then be able to replicate the feeling and "give back" to you. If you give them dedication, they will respond with enthusiasm. If you give them attention, the answer will be motivation. If you give them love, you will eventually receive love, appreciation, and astounding results in your class. Your students will learn and develop as individuals. You will also learn, grow, and become a better teacher as well. Trust me, this is an experience that you will not forget and it will remind you of the amazing power of education and the sublime feeling that comes with being a teacher.

MARVELOUS LOVE

When I think about the importance of love in our learning communities, one student stands out in my mind—let's call him John. John was angry, rebellious, and always seemed to be on the verge of exploding. He would come into class with a chip on his shoulder, and it seemed he was always ready to pick a fight. At first, I didn't know how to handle John. I tried to reason with him and show him that I cared, but nothing seemed to work. Then, one day, I had an idea. Instead of trying to change John, I decided to try to understand him.

I pulled John aside one day after class and asked him what was happening. He opened up and told me how he felt rejected, hated, and unappreciated. He felt like no one cared about him and that he was all alone in the world. I realized that he wasn't just angry—he was hurting.

So, I decided to make an effort to make him feel seen, heard, and loved. I would check in, ask him how he was doing, and listen to what he had to say. I tried acknowledging his strengths and accomplishments and letting him know I believed in him.

As I did this, something started to shift in John. He began to soften, to let down his guard, and to show signs of vulnerability. He started to open up to his classmates and even began to form some new friendships in class!

Looking back on that experience, I realize I had learned an important lesson. Sometimes, the best way to help a problematic student is to approach them with compassion and empathy. It's not about changing or fixing them but about understanding and making them feel seen, heard, and loved.

In the end, I not only helped John, but I also grew as a teacher. I realized that teaching is about more than just imparting knowledge. Building relationships and helping students find their place in the world are equally important. In some cases, establishing meaningful relationships is even more important to a student in the long run. And that's what I strive to do every day.

As you move on to the conclusion, I want you to take a moment and reflect on everything that you have learned so far. Think about the steps we have gone through and the methods that you have seen that can help you once again see the marvelous world of education. That you have found meaning and significance in what was written here and that this book has, in some way, helped you identify solutions to the problems that are present daily in our classrooms. That you have recovered motivation and feel like it **is** possible to change the scenario of what our education system looks like. That it's possible to get rid of the toxicity that fills our schools and showing our students that education is wonderful.

Invite other teachers to inspire their students by motivating themselves first!

You now have a host of new strategies to employ in your class to make each and every student feel seen and heard. You know what it takes to awe students, engage them in meaningful dialogue, and turn your classroom into a haven of love and connection.

Simply by sharing your honest opinion of this book on Amazon, you'll show other teachers where they can find the guidance they need.

Thank you so much for your support. I wish you the best of luck on your journey as an educator.

Scan the QR code below

STEPPING INTO YOUR MARVELOUS FUTURE

As we end this book, it's important to remember the key points we've discussed. First and foremost, building solid relationships with your students is the foundation of effective classroom management. By observing and listening to your students, you can better understand their needs and motivations and create a positive and engaging learning environment.

But more is needed to build relationships with your students. You also need to make learning meaningful and inspiring for them. That means going beyond delivering content, to connect with your students more profoundly. By helping them see the relevance and value of what they're learning, you can foster a sense of wonder and curiosity that will stay with them for years.

To truly transform your classroom, moving beyond content delivery and establishing a deep connection with your students is crucial. By helping them recognize the relevance and value of their learning, you can unlock their boundless curiosity and unleash their limitless creativity. You can unleash their curiosity and creativity in ways you never thought possible by helping them see the relevance and value of what they're learning.

Of course, putting these strategies into practice can be challenging. That's why I've included practical tips and techniques that you can use to overcome challenges and achieve success. By following these proven methods, you'll be able to create a classroom environment that supports learning, growth, and happiness for everyone involved.

But don't just take my word for it. I've seen countless success stories from teachers who have implemented these strategies in their own classrooms and witnessed the incredible impact they can have on their students' lives. By adopting these techniques and continuing to learn and grow as a teacher, you, too, can make a profound difference in the lives of your students.

So, as you move forward on your journey toward becoming an extraordinary teacher, remember that the power to inspire and transform lives is within your grasp. You can create a classroom that genuinely marvels with passion, dedication, and a willingness to learn and grow.

Your students may not all become rocket scientists. They might not even go into higher education because of the path they have chosen in their lives. But you will know, deep inside, that you have done your best to help them and show them purpose. That you have really given your best in each and every one of the classes that you have taught. You have helped these students marvel at the idea that they can be their own heroes, the changing catalyst of their lives. You will have been what I have mentioned from the very beginning that you can and must be: The driver of change.

There is a solution, you have seen it and I am here to tell you that it is possible. Change is within your reach and now it is up to you to give it a try. I have full confidence that you are able to do it, and that you will see your students thrive in the classroom and find significance. That you will find the path to helping these students onto their journey and take some of the burden you carry off your shoulders.

My hopes for you, as you finish reading this book, is that you have reconnected with the reasons why you became an educator. That the book helps you reignite the fire and find the motivation you were lacking. That you do not give up hope that things can change and be different by being the driving factor of change.

Lastly, I want to mention that this is the first in a series of educational books with the objective of helping teachers understand how they can positively impact the classroom. Each of the books will feature a different perspective and methods that I have successfully applied and seen the results from in the classroom. This is just the beginning!

I want to ask that if you feel this book has made a significant impact in your life as a teacher, and helped you find alternatives to problems that seemed to have no solutions, you let others know by leaving a review. If I have been able to help you, I hope I can do the same for other teachers who are beginning their journey into education and feel hopeless and lost with the lack of support.

I wish you the best of luck in your journey and hope you are as excited as I am about the changes that are about to occur. I hope you have been able to go back and reach into that place inside you that made you become a teacher in the first place. Remember: You can do it. So go forth and make a difference! It is never late to inspire marvel and be marvelous.

REFERENCES

Albert Einstein quotes. (n.d.). BrainyQuote. https://www.brainyquote.com/quotes/albert_einstein_121255

Allen, S. (2018, September 26). *Eight reasons why awe makes your life better.* Greater Good. https://greatergood.berkeley.edu/article/item/eight_reasons_why_awe_makes_your_life_better

A quote by Robert Frost. (n.d.). Goodreads. https://www.goodreads.com/quotes/50818-i-am-not-a-teacher-but-an-awakener

A quote by William Glasser. (n.d.). Goodreads. https://www.goodreads.com/quotes/156710-when-you-study-great-teachers-you-will-learn-much-more

Aran, R. (2017, June 17). *Why do we ask questions?* Medium. https://romyaran1.medium.com/why-do-we-ask-questions-c03490e44756

Aristotle Quotes About Teaching. A-Z Quotes, https://www.azquotes.com/author/524-Aristotle/tag/teaching. Accessed 17 May 2023

Bagnall, V. (2023). *"The Power of Myth" by Joseph Campbell with Bill Moyers.* YouTube. https://www.youtube.com/watch?v=6IeTx1RkCsk

Bidshahri, R. (2017, December 4). *Let me blow your mind: The importance of awe in education.* Singularity Hub. https://singularityhub.com/2017/12/04/let-me-blow-your-mind-the-importance-of-awe-in-education/

Bolland, P. (2021). *The Four Functions of Myth.* YouTube. https://www.youtube.com/watch?v=WqaN3rWjyCc

Campbell, J. (2004). *Pathways to Bliss: Mythology and Personal Transformation.* New World Library.

Carnegie Mellon University. (2019). *Students lack interest or motivation.* https://www.cmu.edu/teaching/solveproblem/strat-lackmotivation/index.html

Center for Deployment Psychology. (n.d.). *Socratic Dialogue.* Uniformed Services University. https://deploymentpsych.org/content/socratic-dialogue

Chen, A. (2018, July 18). *How we create personal myths, and why they matter.* Catapult. https://catapult.co/stories/column-data-stories-we-tell-about-ourselves-and-why-they-matter

Cherry, K. (2022, May 23). *Motivation: Psychological factors that guide behavior.*

Verywell Mind. https://www.verywellmind.com/what-is-motivation-2795378

Christie, N. (2009, September 27). *The great aim of education is not knowledge but action. Herbert Spencer.* Make a Change Blog. https://www.nancychristie.com/makeachange/2009/09/the-great-aim-of-education-is-not-knowledge-but-action-herbert-spencer/

Chuter, C. (2020, January 20). *The Role of Motivation in Learning.* The Education Hub. https://theeducationhub.org.nz/motivation/

Cierchia, M. (n.d.). *The Importance of Motivation For Kids.* Touch-Type Read and Spell (TTRS). https://www.readandspell.com/importance-of-motivation-for-kids

Crotty, J. M. (2013, March 13). *Motivation Matters: 40 percent of High School Students Chronically Disengaged From School.* Forbes. https://www.forbes.com/sites/jamesmarshallcrotty/2013/03/13/motivation-matters-40-of-high-school-students-chronically-disengaged-from-school

Cullins, A. (2022, August 23). *How to Explain Growth Mindset to Kids: Neuroplasticity Activities.* Big Life Journal. https://biglifejournal.com/blogs/blog/teach-kids-growth-mindset-neuroplasticity-activities

Dastagir, A. E. (2021, June 7). *Awe Makes Us Happier, Healthier and Humbler.* USA TODAY. https://eu.usatoday.com/story/life/health-wellness/2021/06/07/awe-has-health-benefits-our-wellbeing-how-add-your-life/7586396002/

Delic, H., & Bećirović, S. (2016). Socratic Method as an Approach to Teaching. *European Researcher, 111*(10). https://doi.org/10.13187/er.2016.111.511

Dickinson, K. (2021, November 3). *The Awesome Power of Awe: How This Neglected Emotion Can Change Lives.* Big Think. https://bigthink.com/the-learning-curve/awe/

DiGiulio, S. (2019, February 19). *Why Scientists Say Experiencing Awe Can Help You Live Your Best Life.* NBC News. https://www.nbcnews.com/better/lifestyle/why-scientists-say-experiencing-awe-can-help-you-live-your-ncna961826

Dislen, G. (2013). The Reason of Lack of Motivation From the Students' and Teachers' Voices. *The Journal of Academic Social Sciences, 1*(1), 35–35. https://doi.org/10.16992/asos.13

Drury, P. (2019, March 14). *The Four Functions of Myth and How They Apply to Personal Branding.* Medium. https://patchdrury.medium.com/the-four-functions-of-myth-and-how-they-apply-to-personal-branding-c890d5eea1f9

Drury, P. (2020, May 31). *The Four Functions of Mythology*. Medium. https://patchdrury.medium.com/the-four-functions-of-mythology-f3a4708986c2

Dwight D. Eisenhower quotes. (n.d.). BrainyQuote. https://www.brainyquote.com/quotes/dwight_d_eisenhower_149102

Espel, E. (2022, September 2). *How the Brain Grows, Neuroplasticity Elementary Students*. Empowering Education. https://empoweringeducation.org/blog/how-the-brain-grows/

Exeed College. (2019, July 1). *Role of Teachers in Education*. Exeed College. https://exeedcollege.com/blog/the-role-of-teachers-in-education/

Ferreira, M., Cardoso, A. P., & Abrantes, J. L. (2011). Motivation and Relationship of the Student with the School as Factors Involved in the Perceived Learning. *Procedia - Social and Behavioral Sciences, 29,* 1707–1714. https://doi.org/10.1016/j.sbspro.2011.11.416

Fitzpatrick, L. (2018, January 16). *Teaching Curiosity Through Responding with Wonderment and Awe*. ASCD. https://www.ascd.org/blogs/teaching-curiosity-through-responding-with-wonderment-and-awe

Flippen Group. (2016, August 3). *For Too Many Students, School is the One Place They Receive Love*. Flippen Group. https://flippengroup.com/for-too-many-students-school-is-the-one-place-they-receive-love/

Flynn, B. (2021, June 30). *The Hero's Journey Stages and Structure*. Skillshare Blog. https://www.skillshare.com/en/blog/the-heros-journey-stages-and-structure/

Ford, V. B., & Roby, D. E. (n.d.). *Why Do High School Students Lack Motivation in the Classroom?* (pp. 101–113) [Thesis]. https://libres.uncg.edu/ir/uncp/fWhy

Garrett Izzo, David. *The Great Yearning: The Perennial Philosophy as a Literary Theory with Examples from Modern Literature*. Diss. The Temple University Graduate Board, 2005.

Goldstein, L. S. (2003). The Pedagogical Power of Myth in Teacher Education. *The Journal of Educational Thought (JET) / Revue de La Pensée Éducative, 37*(2), 157–176. https://www.jstor.org/stable/23767413

GreatSchools Staff. (2022, November 16). *Motivating the Unmotivated Student*. https://www.greatschools.org/gk/articles/motivating-the-unmotivated-student/

Greenberg, J., Putman, H., & Walsh, K. (2014, January). *Training Your Future*

Teachers: Classroom Management. National Council on Teacher Quality. https://www.nctq.org/dmsView/Future_Teachers_Classroom_Management_NCTQ_Report

Harris, R. (2023, March 1). *43+ teacher burnout statistics of 2023 (reasons & hours)*. NutMeg Education. https://nutmegeducation.com/teacher-burnout-statistics

Hawthorne, H. (2021, November 17). *Types of Motivation in Education*. High Speed Training. https://www.highspeedtraining.co.uk/hub/motivation-in-education/

Hehe, J. (2021, September 21). *Socratic Debate*. Medium. https://joshuashawnmichaelhehe.medium.com/socratic-debate-b7800b1b817d

Hillary. (2023, March 2). *Five Reasons You Should Embrace Awe in Your Life*. Transitioning Your Life. https://www.transitioningyourlife.com/five-reasons-you-should-embrace-awe-in-your-life/

Holiday, M. (2018, October 16). *What To Do When Your Students Won't Listen*. Feed Their Needs. https://www.feedtheirneeds.com/students-wont-listen/

Hough, L. (2018). *What's Love Got To Do With It?* Harvard Graduate School of Education. https://www.gse.harvard.edu/sites/default/files/edmag/pdfs/2018-FAL-6.pdf

Hulleman, C. S., & Hulleman, T. (2018, January 10). *An Important Piece of the Student Motivation Puzzle*. FutureEd. https://www.future-ed.org/reversing-the-decline-in-student-motivation/

Indeed. (2023, January 27). *The Socratic Method of Teaching: Definition, Benefits and Tips*. https://www.indeed.com/career-advice/career-development/socratic-method-teaching

Irving, S. (2019, February 24). *The Importance of Awe*. Medium. https://medium.com/@sjirving1987/the-importance-of-awe-9ff6b1fc9c63

Jo. (2014, November 26). *Learning requires exploration of one's identity*. First Peoples Principles of Learning. https://firstpeoplesprinciplesoflearning.wordpress.com/learning-requires-exploration-of-ones-identity/

Joseph Campbell Foundation. (2022). *The Center Of The World*. YouTube. https://www.youtube.com/watch?v=irQ30klqAYE

Koehler, J. (2023, March 18). *11 benefits of experiencing awe in childhood*. Psychology Today. https://www.psychologytoday.com/us/blog/beyond-school-walls/202303/11-benefits-of-experiencing-awe-in-childhood

Kuurme, T., & Carlsson, A. (2012). The Importance and Meaning of Learning at School in Students' Consciousness. *International Education Studies, 5*(4). https://doi.org/10.5539/ies.v5n4p166

Lack of Motivation in Students and the Possible Reasons Behind It. (2009, November 9). Eduzenith. https://eduzenith.com/lack-of-motivation-in-students

Lattimer, C. (2020, January 7). *6 Reasons Why Being Motivated Is Not Enough.* The People Development Magazine. https://peopledevelopmentmagazine.com/2020/01/07/being-motivated-is-not-enough/

Livni, E. (2018, October 26). *This Classic Formula Can Show You How to Live More Heroically.* Quartz. https://qz.com/1436608/this-classic-formula-can-show-you-how-to-live-more-heroically

Llego, M. A. (2022, September 16). *The Socratic Method: A Powerful Tool For Your Classroom.* TeacherPH. https://www.teacherph.com/socratic-method-classroom/

Loar, C. (2010, October 28). *The Meaning of Life: "Joseph Campbell on the Power of Myth With Bill Moyers."* PopMatters. https://www.popmatters.com/132546-joseph-campbell-on-the-power-of-myth-with-bill-moyers-2496120081.html

Master Class. (n.d.). *What is the Hero's Journey?* https://www.masterclass.com/articles/writing-101-what-is-the-heros-journey

McAdams, D. P., & McLean, K. C. (2013). Narrative Identity. *Current Directions in Psychological Science, 22*(3), 233–238. https://www.jstor.org/stable/44319052?read-now=1#page_scan_tab_contents

McGee, G. Z. (2018, September 9). *Joseph Campbell's Four Basic Functions of Mythology.* Fractal Enlightenment. https://fractalenlightenment.com/36315/life/joseph-campbells-four-basic-functions-of-mythology

McKimmie, B. (2021, October 27). *Purposefully Building Identity and Belonging Among Students.* The Higher Times Education. https://www.timeshighereducation.com/campus/purposefully-building-identity-and-belonging-among-students

Mclean, K. C., & Pasupathi, M. (2010). *Narrative Development in Adolescence: Creating the Storied Self.* Springer. https://dl.uswr.ac.ir/bitstream/Hannan/139352/1/9780387898247.pdf

Meredith. (2019, August 22). *4 Reasons Why Your Students Aren't Listening to You (and what to do about it).* A Waldorf Journey. https://www.awaldorfjourney.com/2019/08/4-reasons-why-your-students-arent-listening-to-you-and-what-to-do-about-it/

Metz, T. (2021, February 9). *The Meaning of Life.* Stanford. https://plato.stanford.edu/entries/life-meaning/

Miller, D. (2011, March). *What Makes a Hero?* Walb News. https://www.walb.com/story/14157521/special-report-what-makes-a-hero/

Miller, R. (2021, November 11). *Using the Socratic Method in Your Classroom.* Edutopia. https://www.edutopia.org/article/using-socratic-method-your-classroom/

Mr. Mustafa. (2023a, February 6). *10 Reasons Why Your Students Don't Listen to You (and how you can fix it).* Teacher How. https://teacherhow.com/reasons-why-your-students-dont-listen-to-you/

Mr. Mustafa. (2023b, February 6). *What To Do When a Student Refuses to Listen.* Teacher How. https://teacherhow.com/what-to-do-when-a-student-refuses-to-listen/

Nguyen, J. (2021, September 8). *Students Want to Be Heard: How a Learning Partnership Conversation Changed My Outlook on "Disruptive" Behavior.* Lead by Learning. https://weleadbylearning.org/2021/09/08/students-want-to-be-heard-how-a-focal-student-conversation-changed-my-outlook-on-disruptive-behavior/

Office of Graduate Studies. (n.d.). *Socratic Questioning.* University of Nebraska-Lincoln. https://graduate.unl.edu/connections/socratic-questioning

Padma. (2014, September 22). *7 Reasons Why Asking Questions Helps Learning.* The Teacher's Digest. http://theteachersdigest.com/7-reasons-why-asking-questions-helps-learning/

Phillips, E. (2022, November 3). *How to Manage Attention-Seeking Behaviour in Your Students.* The Will to Teach. https://willtoteach.com/how-to-manage-attention-seeking-behaviour-in-school-students/

Rademacher, T. (2015, March 27). *Our Students Are Talking But We're Not Listening.* Ed Post. https://www.edpost.com/stories/our-students-are-talking-but-were-not-listening

Reis, R. (2021, July 23). *The Socratic Method: What it is and How to Use it in the Classroom.* Quadrat Academy. https://www.quadratacademy.com/single-post/the-socratic-method-what-it-is-and-how-to-use-it-in-the-classroom

Resilient Educator. (2012, November 7). *Socratic Method of Teaching: Pros and Cons.* https://resilienteducator.com/classroom-resources/should-educators-use-the-socratic-method-of-teaching/

Riddell, P., & McDermott, I. (2014, August 15). *How Neuroscience Can Improve*

Strategic Questioning. World of Learning. https://www.learnevents.com/learning-insights/how-neuroscience-can-improve-strategic-questioning/

Robinson, K. (2006). Do Schools Kill Creativity? *YouTube*. https://www.youtube.com/watch?v=iG9CE55wbtY

Rudd, M., Hildebrand, C., & Vohs, K. D. (2018). Inspired to Create: Awe Enhances Openness to Learning and the Desire for Experiential Creation. *Journal of Marketing Research, 55*(5), 766–781. https://www.jstor.org/stable/26966540

Saint Leo University. (2022, October 12). *The Socratic method of teaching: What it is, its benefits, and examples | Saint Leo University*. https://www.saintleo.edu/about/stories/blog/socratic-method-teaching-what-it-its-benefits-and-examples

Schadt, S. (2021, January 27). *Socratic Questions*. University of Connecticut. https://cetl.uconn.edu/resources/teaching-your-course/leading-effective-discussions/socratic-questions/

Schuon, F. (1999). *Dimensions of Islam* (P. N. Townsend, Trans.). London, Allen & Unwin.

Sheninger, E. (2016, June 27). *Inspiring students: Bringing Awe Back to Learning*. A Principal's Reflections. https://esheninger.blogspot.com/2016/06/inspiring-students-bringing-awe-back-to.html

Silva, V. (2019, July 22). *10 Reasons Your Child May Have No Motivation to Study*. Built by Me - STEM Learning. https://www.builtbyme.com/no-motivation-to-study-reasons/

Silvia, P. (2012). *Knowledge Emotions: Feelings That Foster Learning, Exploring, and Reflecting*. Noba. https://nobaproject.com/modules/knowledge-emotions-feelings-that-foster-learning-exploring-and-reflecting

Sima, R. (2022, September 15). Why it is awesome that your brain can experience awe. *Washington Post*. https://www.washingtonpost.com/wellness/2022/09/15/awe-mental-health/

SJPAS Inter College. (2022, January 20). *The Importance of Motivation in Student Life*. https://sjpasintercollege.in/the-importance-of-motivation-in-student-life/

Smith, B. (2012). *What is Awe?* GoStrengths. https://gostrengths.com/what-is-awe/

Smith, M. (2022, November 22). *"It killed my spirit": How 3 teachers are navigating the burnout crisis in education*. CNBC. https://www.cnbc.com/2022/

11/22/teachers-are-in-the-midst-of-a-burnout-crisis-it-became-intolerable.html

Smit, J. (n.d.). The Role of Mythology in Education. In *Waldorf Library* (pp. 9–19). https://www.waldorflibrary.org/images/stories/Journal_Articles/WJP16mythology.pdf

Socrates quotes. (2018). Goodreads. https://www.goodreads.com/author/quotes/275648.Socrates

Souders, B. (2019, November 5). *What is Motivation? A Psychologist Explains*. Positive Psychology. https://positivepsychology.com/what-is-motivation/

Spainhour, K. (n.d.). Neuroplasticity and the Whole Child Approach to Teaching. *N2Y*. https://www.n2y.com/wp-content/uploads/neuroplasticity-white-paper.pdf

Steger, M. F., O'Donnell, M. B., & Morse, J. L. (2021). Helping Students Find Their Way to Meaning: Meaning and Purpose in Education. *The Palgrave Handbook of Positive Education*, 551–579. https://doi.org/10.1007/978-3-030-64537-3_22

Stifler, B. (n.d.). *Definition of myth*. https://www.billstifler.org/myth/files/1D-002-definition.htm

Taack Lanier, J. (1997, July 1). *Redefining the Role of the Teacher: It's a Multifaceted Profession*. Edutopia. https://www.edutopia.org/redefining-role-teacher

Taylor, S. (2013, July 21). *The Power of Purpose*. Psychology Today. https://www.psychologytoday.com/intl/blog/out-the-darkness/201307/the-power-purpose

Tarango, T. (2019, November 10). *The Power of Purpose-Based Learning*. Getting Smart. https://www.gettingsmart.com/2019/11/10/the-power-of-purpose-based-learning/

Tarr, T. (2006, March). *Handling Disruptive Student Behavior*. Center for Teaching and Learning. https://ctl.iupui.edu/Resources/Classroom-Management/Tips-for-Handling-Disruptive-Student-Behavior

Terada, Y. (2019, August 7). *8 Proactive Classroom Management Tips*. Edutopia. https://www.edutopia.org/article/8-proactive-classroom-management-tips/

The 7 Roles of a Teacher. (n.d.). Indeed. https://www.indeed.com/hire/c/info/7-roles-of-a-teacher

The Power of Myth Quotes by Joseph Campbell. (2019). Goodreads. https://www.goodreads.com/work/quotes/971052-the-power-of-myth

The Role of Teachers in Education. (2021, April 10). Digital Class Blogs. https://www.digitalclassworld.com/blog/role-of-teacher/

Vianna, E., & Stetsenko, A. (2011). Connecting Learning and Identity Development Through a Transformative Activist Stance: Application in Adolescent Development in a Child Welfare Program. *Human Development, 54*(5), 313–338. https://www.jstor.org/stable/26765017

Vlaicu, C., & Voicu, C. (2013). Supporting Adolescent Identity Development through Personal Narratives. *Procedia - Social and Behavioral Sciences, 92*, 1026–1032. https://doi.org/10.1016/j.sbspro.2013.08.794

Waddington, T. (2009, January 16). *On the Value of Mythologizing Yourself.* Psychology Today. https://www.psychologytoday.com/us/blog/smarts/200901/on-the-value-of-mythologizing-yourself

Walker, T. (2022, February 1). *Survey: Alarming Number of Educators May Soon Leave the Profession | NEA.* National Education Association. https://www.nea.org/advocating-for-change/new-from-nea/survey-alarming-number-educators-may-soon-leave-profession

Weller, D. (2022, September 24). *3 Ways Teachers Can Use the Hero's Journey Framework.* Barefoot TEFL Teacher. https://www.barefootteflteacher.com/p/3-ways-teachers-can-use-the-heros

Why Are Teachers Important in Our Society? Why Teachers Matter. (2019, August 12). University of the People. https://www.uopeople.edu/blog/the-importance-of-teachers/

Why Is Asking and Answering Questions Important? (2018, March 29). ABC Pediatric Therapy. https://www.abcpediatrictherapy.com/why-is-asking-and-answering-questions-important/

Zakrzewski, V. (2013, June 11). *How Awe Can Help Students Develop Purpose.* Greater Good Magazine. https://greatergood.berkeley.edu/article/item/how_awe_can_help_students_develop_purpose

Printed in the USA
CPSIA information can be obtained
at www.ICGtesting.com
LVHW071737091123
763515LV00009B/146